stop
worrying
about
money

stop worrying about money

start planning now to secure your financial future

Jacqui Clarke

WILEY

First published in 2023 by John Wiley & Sons Australia, Ltd
Level 4, 600 Bourke St, Melbourne Victoria 3000, Australia.

Typeset in Lora 10pt/15pt

© John Wiley & Sons Australia, Ltd 2023

The moral rights of the author have been asserted

ISBN: 978-1-394-17688-5

A catalogue record for this book is available from the National Library of Australia

Cover design by Wiley

Disclaimer
The material in this publication is of the nature of general comment only, and does not represent professional advice. It is not intended to provide specific guidance for particular circumstances and it should not be relied on as the basis for any decision to take action or not take action on any matter which it covers. Readers should obtain professional advice where appropriate, before making any such decision. To the maximum extent permitted by law, the author and publisher disclaim all responsibility and liability to any person, arising directly or indirectly from any person taking or not taking action based on the information in this publication.

Printed in Singapore
M124234_070223

Contents

About the author

Jacqui Clarke could very well be Australia's best-kept money secret.

Over her 30-year career, she has been a trusted advisor and accountant to some of Australia's most iconic and wealthy families. What she has learned is that we all worry about money — no matter how much we actually have!

For most of us, money is a complex world of relationships and expectations. This is why Jacqui takes the emotion out of finance for those 'too close to it', 'too busy' or simply 'too confused'.

She is a truthsayer: a conscience and a confidant to clients, family and peers, helping them navigate their financial future with confidence.

To Jacqui, managing money comes pretty naturally. At the age of 10, she would take customer bookings for her family's building and plumbing business. It was very clear to her that someone had to be across the details in business and that, more importantly, everybody needed a trusted expert. This belief has carried Jacqui through her career and is an integral part of this book.

An accomplished executive and business professional, including more than 20 years with Deloitte, Jacqui has held executive roles across Australia, New Zealand and Asia in industries and sectors including retail, property, automotive, professional services, technology, financial services, agriculture, and oil and gas.

She spent two highly successful decades as a full services executive, including time as Head of Clients and Brand, and then went on to co-found Maxima Private, a boutique accounting and advisory firm. Through its virtual family office program, Maxima Private helps families manage, grow and protect their wealth. Jacqui's consulting business is where she focuses on her trusted advisor role for boards and families.

Jacqui is the chair of an iconic global family business, and non-executive director on two ASX-listed boards and a charity. She is also a fellow of the Institute of Chartered Accountants Australia and New Zealand (CAANZ), a graduate of the Australian Institute of Company Directors (AICD), a chartered tax advisor, a fellow of the Taxation Institute of Australia and a Justice of the Peace.

Her hope for you through this book is to see that money allows you to enjoy life, but it also comes with great responsibility. With careful planning and effort, you can manage your money so it doesn't manage you.

jacquiclarke.me

Introduction

Sarah is a busy professional with huge responsibilities at home and work. As a partner in a large professional services firm, she often multitasks at work. The demands seem tireless: putting out little fires here and there, and responding to a myriad emails and demands on her time.

It doesn't stop when Sarah leaves the office. In fact, prior to arriving at work each day, she has already been for a morning run, had breaky and sent the kids off to school. Rushing is the norm; the end of the day, not unlike the start, seems like madness. Groceries to grab on the way home, talking with the kids about their school day, working out who needs to be where and when. And then her brain is still on at 3 am, churning around thoughts and concerns about which bills need to be paid, or whether the family will have enough money for a holiday this year.

Sarah's husband Paul is also a busy executive in a Big 4 bank. His schedule is equally complex. That means there is a never-ending pile of life admin floating around the house or each of their inboxes. Tax. Permission slips. Doctors' appointments. Holiday planning. Diary coordinating. (Argh! Can you relate?)

The weekends are loaded up with sports for the kids, household chores, cooking. Maybe some entertaining. Little time or thought goes into planning the next day, let alone planning for their future.

Sarah and Paul are an example of your classic time-poor 'wage slaves'. They have good incomes; they are well-qualified and in-demand people. They are smart. *But* this gets in the way of asking for help. Help with money. Help with wealth and living what they think is 'financial freedom'.

They do minimal cash flow planning and bury their money worries. A bonus might come in and it gets spent on a new car, some jewellery, a special handbag, or they might even finally commit to a renovation. Or it might fund their 40th birthday party or a special event with their friends.

It's a cycle of money in, money out.

A treadmill of this kind is okay. Nothing to complain about, right?

But what happens when that treadmill breaks, or you simply want to get off?

Maybe one of you gets sick. Or there's a major corporate shake-up at work. There's a change in strategic direction at one of your firms and you can't stand the 'pressure cooker' any more and want to leave. You add a new family member. You get married. You get divorced. You start a business.

What's been set aside for one of these monumental life changes?

I'm not trying to scare you here, but these things creep up — and usually we're not prepared!

Over the past 10 years, your household income has possibly doubled or even trebled. Yet, coincidentally, there's been a shift — an ever-so-subtle incremental increase — in your expense base. Your lifestyle 'needs' have increased; you might have bought a bigger house, for example. This was a justified move: you needed the space, you had the income to support the bank's loan ratios. You also have some equity in your home now since selling your older place, but you've got a bigger mortgage too.

So, your balance sheet might look good but what income-producing assets do you have (apart from you!)?

The reality for most of us is that the more income we earn, the more frivolous we become. And we're not ready for when shit hits the fan. (Hello, pandemic.) And all this adds up to worry, which compounds over time.

The good news is that you can do something about this.

You can control your finances and build a plan to secure your financial future.

You can turn around your balance sheet. You can turn your relationship with money into a more practical, positive and useful tool to get what you really want from life. To plan strategically for you and your family's future. To protect and preserve it and share your money in a consistent and fulfilling way, without adding more stress and anxiety.

I know this because I've done it many times, for myself as well as others like you.

Over the past three decades I've worked with people from a wide variety of backgrounds, including some of Australia's and Asia's richest families. I've learned a few money tricks along the way and I've observed a lot of money traps: the windfall gains, the business sales, the promotions, the overseas moves.

I've been divorced; remarried; blended a family with five sons (step-parenting takes being a parent to a new level of complexity); left my 'executive' career; and established, bought and sold businesses and so much more.

No matter where you are at right now, you have the ability to worry less about money and plan a secure future.

Notwithstanding setbacks, you can build and re-build a more enduring positive relationship with money along the way.

Money matters plague too many relationships! Executive editor at *Mamamia* Leigh Campbell said on her *Out Loud* podcast that in her friendship circles 'every single couple that are separated or divorced had separate finances'. It begs the question: do you run big-ticket spending items by your spouse? Should you? We'll unpack these common questions together in the chapters ahead.

This book is a culmination of my experience and insights gained from 50 years on this planet and more than 30 years advising and observing people like you.

At a time when our trust in financial services and scammers is at an all-time low, this book serves as a trusted sounding board for life's misadventures and adventures.

You'll find the tools and skills you need to:

- take control of your money and avoid the typical money traps
- master the art of planning with money and create personal accountability
- make empowered money decisions
- develop your own plan for financial wellbeing and security
- build a secure financial future to see you through life's ups and downs.

Whether you're building a side-hustle, going through a breakup, blending a family or planning a significant party, you'll learn to work out how to move through your biggest life changes and events, and have fun along the way!

You'll build a wish list for where you're going — for cars, renovations and parties — and you'll see why money isn't *bad*. You just need to get *good* at using it.

Ready?

Jacqui

An important note

Money management is not a set-it-and-forget-it activity. In addition to reading this book you will need to get a little hands-on to ensure you apply the skills and lessons in it.

This book includes practical templates designed to be re-used at different stages on your journey to securing your financial future.

You'll find free downloadable versions of these templates at:

jacquiclarke.me

Keep revisiting these templates and the exercises in this book as your circumstances change or whenever you update your goals.

part I
getting your house in order

The foundation for living a life free of money worries begins with part I.

You need to understand your money story and how events or milestones in your life have impacted your financial baggage.

This can be very challenging for some of us. We'll need to look openly and honestly at all the ugly bits, to dig around in the dirt (or at least dig around for a credit card statement or two). *What hidden spending is there? How are our expenses creeping up?*

Take comfort in knowing that doing these things right and following the activities included with this book will have you on track to set, or re-set, your financial goals so they are better aligned to what you value most.

We'll look at how to build a group of trusted advisors around you without falling prey to the Melissa Caddicks of this world. And then work out what being 'financially free' actually means for you and how you can plan to get there.

Last, but definitely not least, we will look at the uncomfortable but necessary matter of death.

Let's begin.

Chapter 1
Understand your money story

I had what you'd consider a typical middle-class upbringing in the 1980s. I went to a nice school. My father built our house. My parents both had cars. And we enjoyed an annual trip driving somewhere within Australia in summer.

I grew up observing my grandparents and parents running their building and plumbing businesses from home. I saw tradesmen coming and going from the house (or garage) all the time. When I was young, the tradies used to come and pick up their wages, which had been prepared by my mother and placed in a yellow envelope, every Thursday afternoon from the 'office'.

In many respects I had great money role models from the get-go, and that was a blessing. The ethos was simple: work hard; a strong work ethic followed by a 'you can't get ahead without debt' mindset. This has had a significant impact on my life and my money values as debt was considered the norm—to clarify, it was what I'd call 'good debt', such as debt for an investment property or your house, as opposed to credit card debt.

I knew my parents were doing okay, although I do vividly remember the signs of money stress when a long-term client of the business didn't pay their bills. At the time it would have represented more than one-third of their annual income. I'm pretty sure my father preferred working 'in the business' than 'on the business'—that is, he preferred to be hands on rather than doing the admin things like chasing money. So this particular client got away with not paying bills for quite a while. This didn't end well for my family. The client, who had also become a good friend, went bankrupt (turns out we weren't the only ones that hadn't been paid). Needless to say, we never saw a dollar from the work that my father and his team had done over the period of a year or more.

There was little escaping this situation as just about everything was discussed in our kitchen at home, either in person or on the telephone. I know my father felt like he had been conned (for example, the client would regularly tell him that the bills would be paid as soon as X and Y happened). I now reflect on it knowing that the client's business just grew too quickly, and he wasn't managing the outgoings at all. As the bills mounted, the ability to pay them became a test of his storytelling abilities and avoidance techniques. He strung everyone along for a while until the mounting debts were inescapable and he eventually succumbed to bankruptcy due to the inability to pay any of his debts.

This led to my first real money lesson in tightening our belts. It was the first time a conversation like this had landed at our kitchen table: we would all need to make some sacrifices. I recall not taking it too well as a young teen. It felt like a cloud of uncertainty had descended upon us.

My parents had received great advice up front from their accountant on how to fix this. My dad worked six days a week to help us recover from this money setback. The goal at the time was to ensure that the business continued and he could keep his team employed while rebuilding from the loss of income and this meant making some sacrifices on our lifestyle to recoup what had been lost. My mother took on the main role of managing what we spent. Fortunately, the sacrifices were small: my mum paid more attention to the price of items at the supermarket checkout, and a trip to the butcher was a bit more considered, you could say. Her main recollection was that we stopped going out for dinner and we only bought the essentials — nothing more.

This experience influenced and shaped the way I thought and worried about money. It's important to reflect on the stories that have impacted your personal money journey. Ever-so-subtle things like knowing who managed the money when you were growing up; whether your parents ever struggled to pay bills or argued over money; whether they had any debt; whether they discussed money at all. Any number of things (such as experiencing your parents going through divorce) could have impacted you and developed your thinking and understanding about money.

It's important to appreciate and unpack your influences so you can begin to rewrite and adapt your money story to stop worrying about money.

What's your money story?

If you were writing your life CV right now it would no doubt inform your money story. Beginning in your childhood, recording every TV show you watched, every book you've read, the neighbourhood you grew up in, your education and the jobs you've had to this point, will have impacted your money story. These influences, including cultural or generational (grandparents or parents), and the emotions (or lack of) are all intertwined in your money story and provide incredible insight into where you are at now (or how you really got here) and what needs to change to steer you forward to a secure financial future.

Take me, for example. My friends and family will tell you that I wanted to be an accountant from a very early age. It was plainly obvious to me from my experiences in life that everyone needed an accountant in their lives. I have no doubt that the experience of growing up in the business influenced my own desire to understand more and contribute (I decided pretty early on that I wasn't going to be a builder).

I was determined to create my own level of financial independence and wanted to get a job at the age of 14. Fortunately, a close family friend manufactured women's clothing and had a couple of retail outlets. I was chuffed to land my first job (for cash, of course) working in their retail store in the CBD on Thursday nights. I'm pretty sure the commute to and from the CBD took longer than the shift, but I loved every minute of it, and it gave me my first insight into earning an income and having the freedom to spend (or save) it on whatever I wanted. Did you have a similar experience?

Fast forward…I progressed through school, went to university, studied business and promptly got myself a graduate role in an accounting firm. Next I got married, starting working at one of what's now known as the Big 4 (consulting firms), became a partner in the firm and along the way had three amazing sons. Each step along this journey came with increased financial responsibility and financial pressure (aka money worry). I'm sure this sounds familiar.

Not surprisingly, I had created this pressure. I had kicked off my married life living relatively plainly. Our basic needs were all met: food, shelter, medical and of course entertainment. We started out in a two-bedroom flat, sold that to buy a federation house…I mean, a wreck…renovated that not once but twice, then sold it for a much bigger home in a better suburb with a bigger mortgage. I had gone from owning a typical Australian sedan to leasing a fancy European car. Our trips to the south coast of New South Wales were superseded by trips overseas. We drank nice wine. Each time I received a pay increase or promotion we would increase our cost of living, and experienced our very own expense creep.

More income, more debt, more expenses…

At each one of these life stages I was often faced with money decisions and choices, although I was always pretty focused on earning more and also wanting to build financial security. This all came to a grinding halt when I went through a very difficult divorce. I was pretty comfortable financially at the time (and I knew what money was coming in and going out). I was the one who managed our money, so I was across all the ins and outs (I don't think many people could say that). But divorce rocked my financial security like few things can.

Was there a moment in your life when your money story took a U-turn?

By the time we had finished in court, all the money I had saved and put into my home since my first job at 14 years of age was *gone*.

Any battle and any court interaction is expensive, especially one over a property settlement. As the sole breadwinner, I was expected to provide my soon-to-be ex-husband with the same standard of living to which he had been accustomed. I'm oversimplifying, of course. But you wouldn't wish this process on anyone. (Avoid court wherever possible — more on this in chapter 7). Basically, we landed on a split financially (of the remaining assets) well in my ex-husband's favour so that we could go our separate ways. Admittedly, the reason for the financial split did make sense: I had a job (he was a stay-at-home dad) and I was earning good money. It was tough to accept at the time though. I also made a very significant 'call' during the process and that was to end the process. I asked my lawyers to forgo a greater percentage of our remaining assets to avoid fighting an even longer battle in court, which would have shrunk what remained of our combined wealth.

So, on my journey to 40 I was starting over again. (Sigh...)

We need baseline honesty here

Owning your money story is critical, right here and now. Be honest about how you got here; be honest with yourself. What choices did you make or delegate to someone else? Get clear on the good choices: the ones you'd like to replicate over and over. Also get clear on the ones you would have done differently and wouldn't make again. Each layer you peel back defines part of the current shape of your money story and your bad money habits (which I'd like you to let go of once you've banked whatever lesson was embedded in it). Your honesty will inform and enforce what change is required to move ahead.

Honestly, starting again financially was overwhelming at first and I was worried about maintaining some semblance of the lifestyle I had been living. I was solely financially responsible for raising our three young children, which required a significant adjustment to all things money. I was focused on minimising change to the kids' lives wherever possible, and this meant keeping the kids in their school. I was renting for the first time in my life and had to buy all my furniture and belongings again — right down to the vegetable peeler. Foremost in my mind was making my kids feel loved, safe and secure when so much in their worlds had been torn apart.

My stress and anxiety levels were high because I was worried about financial security for my kids if something happened to me. I doubled down on life insurance, TPD (total permanent disablement), trauma and income protection to relieve some of the financial worries I was carrying. I really looked at where I was and where I was going, and that is exactly what I'd like to show you how to do in this chapter.

The only way to rewrite your money story is to be brutally honest about your income and all of your expenses.

I can't emphasise enough, how important it is to recognise the significance of income and expense creep and how we tend to incrementally purchase more expensive items simply because we can. It's important to get on top of this before you become a wage slave to it.

The problem with expense creep is that it happens gradually, almost without you knowing it. As your income rises, you spend a little more, then a little more.

Maybe you eat out rather than eating at home — you know, to celebrate that promotion. Then, with the higher income, you eat out more regularly, maybe once or twice a week. While you're out at dinner, you plan to purchase a new car, one you could never have afforded, but now you can with your higher salary. You buy bottled wine rather than a cask, you eat at even fancier restaurants, you trade up your gym membership for a personal trainer. Rather than flowers or chocolates for your partner you buy a new 'branded' gift — a handbag or a briefcase — and before you even realise, you are on Satan's treadmill of expense creep.

You eventually start to commit to costs in anticipation of the next pay rise — that is, you commit to spending before you even have the extra money. It's like a disease. When the pay rises stop coming you turn to 'buy now, pay later' so you can commit to the new TV. Surely next year there will be another pay rise, or you can do some overtime — right?

In my case, I had always been comfortable doing the household budget and needed to maintain this practice now more than ever. But there was no denying I had fallen into this common trap of income and expense creep. Our lifestyle cost had exploded as my income grew. So, starting again was a great big wake-up call! I needed to create headroom, to work out how to save again, to recognise there were new costs to consider — for example, a nanny (or house manager, as we called them). If I was to re-shape my financial future and eventually buy a house again, I could not ignore the expense creep — no blind eyes. My goal was to eventually find a home that I could buy for my sons and me. My initial goal was to keep them in the school they were at.

Before we turn this around to look closely at you and your unique situation and story, I want you to know that even to this day, I keep a running spreadsheet that adds up what it costs to run our house. This is a must-do. It's much easier to manage and get in control of what you know than to stay in a continual cycle of expense creep (more like expense oblivion).

Money worries will be perpetual if you don't own your expenses and recognise the outgoings from your house.

Understanding your income and expenses properly is a way of easing your anxiety, no matter what situation you find yourself in.

As time went on, I remarried. My partner, Michael, brought his two sons into our family. He had similarly arrived with no assets post an expensive divorce, so again all of our income, costs and expenses changed — and so too did our goals.

There we were, two adults, five sons (all in private schools) managing a very big mortgage as we basically had nothing to put down (we were fortunate the banks considered our joint incomes as enough security). We had a full-time 'house manager' because we were both working like crazy. We needed all the help we could get. Initially, we leased cars to drive. It was hardcore but at the same time we were backing ourselves and our financial future — and careers — to eventually create headroom, to get into a place where we could see a little bit of equity build up in our house. The only way we could do this was by analysing the costs of 'opening our front door'.

'Open your front door'

Now it's your turn. Taking stock of three critical money items in the steps that follow will have you well on track to developing a baseline towards cost understanding and management. This is just the initial stage; these three money items are the building blocks of the journey to financial security and towards a future with a whole lot less worry. They are:

1. understanding and recognising your expense creep (an honest challenge)

2. analysing your 'open the front door' costs

3. creating your *new* baseline.

Let's look at each in turn.

1. Understand and recognise your expense creep

Let's begin with a high-level evaluation of your money story using some questions. This will also help identify where you may have overstretched recently. Take a minute to consider these (using the last five years as a sample):

- Are you a spendthrift (over spender)?
- Do you purchase things now that require you to make payments in the future?
- Have you battled to save money?
- Have your family/parents helped you financially in any way?
- Did you receive a pay rise and buy something new?
- Have you ever received a tax refund and splurged it straight away on something?
- Have you upsized your house and mortgage?
- Have you bought or leased a new car?
- Do you go to fancy restaurants more than the local pizza or fish and chips shop?
- Do you select the more expensive grocery items, or buy from a local boutique grocer versus a big grocery chain?
- Do you buy more than you need or use?
- Have you got more than one or two streaming service subscriptions?
- Do you ignore your own budget or not have one?

If you answered yes to a number of these, you might be in need of some assistance with taming your expense creep or at least getting your baseline sorted.

Consider how you can avoid the trap of earning more and spending more. It's easy to get bound up in the work treadmill (or hamster

(continued)

11

wheel) and not realise the impact of the ever-expanding choice associated with your increasing income.

It's fair to say that we all have expectations of our lifestyles, maybe like the one you had growing up that informed your money story, and how you responded. You can change it or match it, but you don't need to fall into the same patterns if your income doesn't permit it.

2. Analyse your monthly 'open the front door' costs

Next, let's look at easing your anxiety about common expense items. Dig out any bank account statements you have, and grab your last credit card statement and any bills, such as electricity. We're going to list them all out and add them up.

Some of the expenses listed in the table may be paid quarterly or annually. Locate them and add them to this list as the fraction representative for one month.

In the middle column, scribble down the number, and total it when you get to the end. (I'll explain the purpose of the final column further down.)

There are a few blank lines for you to enter any special or unique costs you have in your house.

Open your front door (tier 1)	Monthly ($)	To be reviewed
Rent or mortgage payment		
Electricity		
Gas		
Water		

Open your front door (tier 1)	Monthly ($)	To be reviewed
Council rates		
Strata levies		
Mobile phone monthly fees		
Home internet		
Subscriptions		
– Apple		
– Amazon		
– Netflix, Stan, Paramount, Apple TV +		
– Spotify or other music source		
Cloud storage		
Home and contents insurance		
Health insurance		
Food (one of the biggest bills in our house!)		
Car running costs such as petrol and oil		
Other		

(continued)

Open your front door (tier 1)	Monthly ($)	To be reviewed
Open your front door sub-total (1)	$	

Now add to these some of your annual costs divided by 12 to give you a monthly amount.

Open your front door (tier 1)	Annual cost / 12 ($)	To be reviewed
Car rego and CTP		
Car insurance		
Memberships		
Pest control		
Glasses		

Open your front door (tier 1)	Annual cost / 12 ($)	To be reviewed
Open your front door sub-total (2)	$	
Total open your front door (tier 1) per month (1 + 2)	$	

Now you know how much it costs to keep the lights on at your place and indeed what costs are associated with you walking in the door.

The recent increase in interest rates and electricity costs, to name just two, may already be putting pressure on your baseline of expenditure and creating another seemingly hidden layer of creep exposure and raising your 'open the front door' costs.

Can you stop the creep?

Look at your list and ask yourself, honestly, the following questions:

- Are these expenses essential?
- Are any of these expenses a want versus a need?
- Are any of these items negotiable or are there possible savings (e.g. mortgage interest rate, electricity costs, car insurance)
- Can I re-evaluate or reduce some 'open my front door' costs?
- What trade-offs could I consider?
- What's missing?

Asking yourself these questions is helping flex your current money story. Rather than setting and forgetting any long-term expense creep, you are now challenging your 'open the front door' costs to stop them expanding like a self-inflating mattress.

When you've got this summary, you can also appreciate that before you go out for a meal, celebrate with a birthday party, buy a new car, take on a new lease or book a holiday you will begin to appreciate what you have to spend before you overspend.

(continued)

3. Create your new baseline

This step requires you to look over your spending in the past year to gather a summary of costs over and above the ones associated with opening your front door. Credit card and bank account scrutiny is required to nail this one.

I like to think of this stage as a wish list. Essentially, you are determining your additional expenses beyond putting that shelter over your head. What are all your other costs or what are the costs that have crept into your life? These are often referred to as 'discretionary expenses' (that is, they're not needed for your survival).

Take the tier 1 total from step 2 and plot it in the middle column at the top of the following table. Then begin to identify all your additional costs—that is, discretionary spending that's not covered in opening your front door.

Very quickly you will be able to see where you can make decisions about keeping or dropping these types of costs. Ideally, once you've plotted all your additional costs you'll be able to decide what to eliminate to create a *new* baseline of costs from where you are today. The sooner you are clear on this, the sooner you can cull 'nice to haves' and focus on planning your secure financial future.

List your additional discretionary annual expenses (A) and then divide these by 12 to arrive at your average monthly baseline expenses (C).

Monthly 'open your front door' (tier 1, from step 2) (A)	$	
Annual baseline expenses (tier 2)	$	To be reviewed
Holidays		

Annual baseline expenses (tier 2)	$	To be reviewed
Entertainment (dinner out/shows/parties / movies (popcorn needs its own expense line))		
Tax return preparation services		
School fees		
Life/trauma/TPD and income protection insurance		
Gym membership or any other sporting costs, e.g. Peloton membership, Pilates, yoga		
Wellness, health and beauty items (massage/ facials/hair)		
Donations		
Clothing		
Parking and tolls		
Ubers		

(continued)

Annual baseline expenses (tier 2)	$	To be reviewed
Total annual baseline expenses	B $	
Average monthly baseline expenses (B/12)	C $	
Total average monthly outgoings and *your* baseline (A + C)	$	

Keep adding to this list by identifying other irregular costs such as:

- renovations
- a new iPhone or laptop
- financial or legal advice
- house repairs from wear and tear
- replacement of large equipment like a dishwasher or fridge
- elective surgery or specialist medical fees.

Has this process given you a feeling that you might need to eliminate some costs now that you realise you've got them? Here are some important points:

- If you are pleasantly surprised (you are in the minority), good for you! But it doesn't mean you're flying high. Keep reading and keep making sense. It's all too easy to fall out of a habit.

- If you are freaked out, you are not alone. Most people will be astounded to know what it costs every single month just to keep their world ticking along without any of the extravagances. The more successful you've been, the worse this experience will be for you.

- If you can't even believe it…welcome to the majority! This is one of the most common reasons for 'worrying' about money. You probably knew it in your gut. If you didn't, you are probably not completely surprised. Expenses go up — and our natural optimism will push them higher and higher without ever having a reality check.

Your response is not the most important part of this exercise. What is important is to get a grasp of what's actually going on.

Go back and reflect on the two lists (your baseline costs), grab a different-coloured pen and in the column headed 'To be reviewed', mark the items that you want to revisit.

Start to identify the things you are prepared to forgo if you have to or the things you are committed to that you wish you had never committed to.

Making sense of the numbers, regularly

There's no question that to arrive at your *new* baseline costs and to reconsider reducing these will require some time. I'd suggest that you need half a day to gather this information (the first time you go about it) and to populate the tables properly. You'll never get ahead unless you know and assess where you've come from and where you're at now, with a goal for where you want to be.

As someone who reviews my 'open the front door' costs regularly I attest to the value of checking these. Occasionally I get little surprises in the process. I received one this week, in fact: a $104.99 fee for UFC (gotta love living in a house with five boys!), and went through the process of having it refunded (after finding out it was an annual fee on auto-renew for a service I wasn't using).

Make this process a habit: getting into a quarterly routine is a good discipline (and will become easier every time).

You want this to be an experience that you look forward to. Be proud that you've nailed the expense creep by reducing the discretionary nice-to-haves to a level that works for you and eases your money worries. In turn, being on top of your outgoings means you won't be overstretched and without any savings directed to your future.

A quick word about budgets

As this is a finance book, you are most likely expecting me to talk about budgets. Personally, I find the exercise that you've just undertaken far more valuable than preparing a budget. It's more tangible, more real and doesn't require any significant financial knowledge — just access to your bank accounts and credit card statements.

Budgets are a helpful *guide* — a forward-looking version of what you've just done — but they aren't the solution to owning your money story (that is, *why* you do the things you do with money). It's critical to understand the past. Looking over your open the front door costs first and then creating your new baseline goes most of the way to creating that much-needed headroom to save and invest for your financial future.

So don't get hung up on doing a budget if you're not into them.

Budgets can be like juice diets: you make a whole bunch of expense-eliminating decisions only to have a real expense blow out when you feel like you need to loosen up a bit — and you're back at square one. Worse, a lot of effort goes into preparing a budget and then you don't look at it again. Or you get a financial surprise, and it blows the budget and disincentivises you to continue. Budgets have a habit of being set once a year and not looked at again.

Taking the approach in steps 1 to 3 of the 'open the front door' exercise will raise your awareness about expenses and expense creep. Following this with your *new* baseline costs can give greater insight into those costs that you need to trim, change or investigate to help work towards your goals and longer term financial security.

Build a new habit into your money story!

Stop worrying now

1. Think about how your parents' or carers' money story might have influenced yours. Do you recall anything about your upbringing that has affected your personal money journey?

2. Be honest with yourself about the money choices you've made. Which ones were good and which ones do you regret? How can you ensure you don't make the same bad choices again?

3. Reflecting on where you're at now, are you spending money on anything that you weren't, say, a year or two ago? If this is discretionary spending, can you find a way of removing it from your baseline?

4. Can you identify your income and expense creep and how it has impacted you? Try to pinpoint where the creep has happened and find ways of reducing its impact—for example, having a birthday gathering at home with family rather than a huge party at a venue might be just as memorable.

Chapter 2
Set meaningful, within-your-means, goals

Life can often seem like an endless series of sliding-door moments — *what if I had done this differently?* You wake up one day and think, *how did I get here?* (C'mon, admit it. I'm sure you've thought that before.) That's why the opportunity to secure your financial future lies in the choice to mindfully set meaningful financial goals as early as possible so you're not always stressing about 'what could have been'.

Whether you've started thinking about taking a year off to travel, home ownership, running your own business or saving for retirement, the sooner you proactively set goals — so you don't feel like you've 'missed out' or left things 'too late' — the more likely you are to achieve them.

A case in point

To help understand why it's important to set goals, and how they will change as life changes, I'd like to share a story about clients of mine,

Bec and Steve, that illustrates how setting meaningful (and within their means) goals early helped them stay focused and on track to securing their financial future.

You'll see that they have had many sliding-door moments where an outcome would have been vastly different (or a poorer choice) if they had stepped through a different door from the one they chose. Having their meaningful goals set helped them stay on track and choose the right door. You will also see how income and expense creep (which we discussed in chapter 1) changed the narrative gradually as lifestyle choices — such as moving to a bigger house, having more kids, and so on — impacted their journey.

Let's take a look at their story to put this into context.

Bec and Steve: setting goals

Bec and Steve were both renting and in their early 30s when they met. While this was working for them in the beginning, as time went on and their relationship developed, it was time for a change. They decided to set a goal to buy their first property together. Their goal was twofold: combine their existing savings and then save jointly in the lead-up to their wedding so they could start married life in their own place.

One of the many considerations was where they would live. They had both been renting close to the CBD for convenience and preferred living closer to the city to reduce the commuting time to and from their CBD jobs. This meant compromising on size because they expected property prices to be much higher than further out.

They took the leap not long after their wedding (with a little kicker from Bec's parents) and settled on a two-bedroom unit with a large, but manageable, mortgage. They were pleased to get into the market because house prices were rising and they worried that holding off any longer could mean they would never afford to get into the market where they wanted to live.

The bank was very thorough with the application for the loan process, and Bec and Steve felt they had to jump through a few hoops, especially with regard to their budget, to assist the bank with assessing their application. Having a good handle on their baseline costs made this a smoother process and also helped them build on their financial literacy by understanding the bank's process for loaning money and how banks take into consideration both income and expenditure.

They knew it would require a bigger commitment of their incomes to pay principal and interest on their 25-year loan as well as a reduction in some of their lifestyle costs. It wasn't the end of their goals—it was really the beginning—so getting their cash-flow right was important and greater attention to living within their means was essential. While they took out a 25-year loan, their expectation was to pay that down as quickly as possible and maybe upsize down the track. They had talked about having children and knew this would make a sizeable dent to their cash flow as they would likely drop to one income for a period of time. Furthermore, they would have the additional costs of raising children, which would directly impact their ability to pay the mortgage.

Baby Jack arrived three years later. Bec took maternity leave for six months, three months of which was paid leave. During the pregnancy, Bec and Steve adjusted their cost of living, continuing to live within their means to ensure they could manage the time at home when the baby arrived. Due to the mortgage and their desire to upsize their home in the not-too-distant future, they decided that Bec should return to the workforce full time. Jack would go into long day care when he was six months old. Adding to cash-flow demands was the cost and location of childcare.

(continued)

They settled on a centre in the CBD so that both Bec and Steve could access it quickly should an emergency arise.

Fast forward and Bec and Steve started contemplating baby number 2 and the need for more space. They'd long outgrown their apartment and started looking for a house. It was the same drill as before, although now they were a bit wiser and more financially literate so the process seemed smoother. Bec and Steve had built up some equity in their apartment and over the previous couple of years the property value had increased. Couple that with increased salaries and of course an increase in the cost of living (and some expense creep too) and they were back at the bank seeking a new loan for a bigger, more expensive home. This time, the trade-off was that they would be living a bit further away from their CBD jobs. They also had to consider the planned second child, meaning some time out of the workforce for Bec, and then double the day-care costs when Bec returned to work.

You can see the complexities for Bec and Steve were increasing. At this time in their life, they had made choices together. They were also maximising their most valuable asset — their income-earning potential — and this was a great time for them to be doing that. (Note: Australian Bureau of Statistics data suggests that between 70 and 90 per cent of our total lifetime income growth occurs in the first 10 years after entering the workforce). I trust you can also see the intersections (and sliding doors) where Bec and Steve made a choice or change that would affect their money story. This would influence the pressure on their income, the pressure on them to work, and the expectations they placed on themselves or others placed on them.

They seemed to have done a good job reassessing their needs and goals and then making changes to their spending. I've kept it simple, but you can appreciate that there were lots of other issues.

Like Bec and Steve, you need to continually reassess your lifestyle, especially when any change happens — for example, a pay rise — and make choices that are aligned with your money goals. In addition, it's important to develop both short-term and long-term goals.

Goals go a long way towards helping you avoid the shiny stuff.

Focus on your future, and be willing to trade

Putting a future lens on your journey is a way to reduce the risk of coming to a screeching halt down the track, when you're older and facing the prospect of having to work the rest of your life because you're likely to enter retirement without savings, or simply coming unstuck because you no longer desire the treadmill effect on your life. I'll admit this is not the typical starting point for any journey to financial enlightenment, but casting your mind forward might be the best way for you to see that something might need to change.

You may also still be staring at the baseline costs you identified in chapter 1, trying to digest the nasty surprise — this can happen, and it's okay if it does. What you know now is valuable and will help project you forward.

Re-evaluating your goals is important as things change in your life or when things are happening to you.

A shift in the global economy, supply problems, labour shortages, a spike in oil prices, inflationary pressure. There's no question there's a nasty list of potential challenges for our baseline costs. No-one can ever say for certain what's ahead, but it's times like these that it pays to take stock of your lifestyle choices and ensure they are structured to withstand what gets thrown your way (such as eight interest rate rises in eight months).

For Bec and Steve, for example, the kids growing up, the need for more space and their desire to reduce the complexity and some of the city pressure on their lives and bank accounts made them consider moving to the country. Since the COVID pandemic, there have been many changes in work habits and day-care arrangements for them both. Needless to say, they are looking at their future financial needs and goals. Like many other families now, reviewing their cost of living in line with their goals has become essential. Paying off a mortgage with increasing interest rates is becoming more difficult and also eating into their discretionary spending.

Even though they are living in the country, there are trade-offs for Bec and Steve. There are fewer choices available for things like retail purchases, but more space and nature. So, their lifestyle has changed. The trade-off may mean less income and it may mean fewer enticing options for how money is spent (fancy restaurants, for example). But again, this may bring them closer to living within their adjusted means.

They may consider cutting expenses such as:

- their planned trip over Christmas
- the number of streaming services they subscribe to
- electricity, by pricing the installation of solar.

Take a moment to consider where you are at. Look at these sliding-door moments and consider the trade-offs that might come with each one:

- holidays (local vs overseas)
- birthday celebrations (party vs family dinner)
- private health insurance (opt in vs opt out)
- education for the kids (public vs private)

- home (bigger house or closer to the city, bigger mortgage)

- city vs country living

- higher income (more demanding job vs current job)

- save for your next egg vs spend now.

Setting both short- and long-term money goals means reflecting on all of the choices we have covered so far. A short-term goal is usually one that you wish to achieve within the next 12 months, whereas a long-term goal could be anytime beyond that: 18 months, three years, five years or even 10 years.

Here are some examples of short- and long-term money goals:

Short-term goals (<12 months)	Long-term goals (>12 months)
Know my 'open the front door' costs	Buy a house
Reset my baseline costs and ensure I know my cost of living	Buy an investment property
Pay off a credit card debt	Cancel or reduce reliance on credit cards
Seek a pay rise or change jobs	Have savings in the bank
Start a new business or side hustle	Buy a holiday house
Celebrate a milestone birthday in style	Save for retirement
Take a holiday	Relocate/upsize or downsize my home
Donate to a charity	Send kids to private schools
Buy a new car	Save to support education for the next generation
Save an extra amount of my income each month	Take a sabbatical or break
Make more money	Need less money

Underpinning your goal setting will be your money values. Just like understanding your money story, knowing what your money values are helps guide your money journey and your goal-setting process. Goals are the specific way you intend to address your money. They are something you aim for. We like goals to be specific — that is, measurable and attainable. Values are more like a compass: they keep you on track...preferably headed in the direction of your goals!

There is a comprehensive goal-setting activity in chapter 10 to assist with all your goals and future vision

What are your money values?

It's easy to see how you can be swept up onto the hamster wheel: expectations from family, your friends, work colleagues or even you yourself can influence money goals and how you stick to them.

So, now is the time to work out what your money values are and how they will enable wise trade-offs towards freedom from stress and anxiety.

Understanding your money values is important for goal setting and when you make choices that are aligned with your values you will feel much more in control of your financial security and future.

Determine your money values

Spend five minutes selecting your top five money values from this list. Then, for those five values, write down how each one applies to you.

Money value	How it applies to you
Living simply (I only need food and shelter)	
Don't need money	
Want a lot of money	
Security	
Healthcare choices	

Money value	How it applies to you
Financial freedom	
Satisfaction	
Building a legacy	
Philanthropy — giving to others	
Lifestyle assets (e.g. a holiday house or boat)	
Fame	
Self-funded retirement	
Being debt free	
High leverage — high ratio of debt to income	
Low debt leverage	
Material possessions	
Luxury items	
Prestige	

Considering what you have selected, are you living an honest life that is true to your values?

(continued)

Look at what you identified and discovered in chapter 1 when you determined what you are spending your hard-earned cash on. Does it all add up or are you frittering away your money on things you don't really value?

It may be time to review your baseline for alignment and to fine-tune your expenditure. Perhaps now is the time to build up your savings buffer to protect you from the unexpected.

Think about what you are adding or subtracting as a part of your go-forward plan.

Being clear on your money values and reviewing these in conjunction with your baseline costs regularly will reduce money worries and give you a feeling of confidence and independence for the longer term.

Stop worrying now

1. What did you learn from identifying your money values?

2. Do you have any financial sliding-door moments ahead of you right now? What will you choose to do and why?

3. Jot down three meaningful short-term money goals.

4. Write down three long-term money goals that are future focused.

5. How would you feel if you achieved these goals?

6. What might you need to change to help you accomplish your goals? And what might you need to trade off to help with this?

Chapter 3

Get to grips with, and in control of, mistakes

As an accountant, I've spent a lot of my career bailing people out — maybe not from jail, but definitely out of the money pit. This is a dark and murky hole that you suddenly realise you've slipped into and can't claw your way out of: spending too much, draining savings, making poor investment decisions, losing income or having to end some kind of relationship.

You might wake in a cold sweat in the middle of the night as your mind meanders through your money worries deliberating things like *Will I run out of money?*, *Can I really afford that?*, *When will these costs ever end?*, *Will I ever get on top of that mortgage?*, *Did I make a mistake buying those shares?*, *What if I get sick?* ... Has this happened to you?

The bottom line — even if you've hit rock bottom — is that you can turn it around. Admitting you've made a mistake or an error of judgement, or that you've just been focused elsewhere, is the best starting point. Your money story up to this point has got you here and you don't need to hold onto your past or doubt yourself further.

Coming to grips with your money mistakes is an important step in getting yourself back on track or indeed on track towards your secure financial future.

Beware the money pit battle

Let's look at how a friend of mine, Nicky, fell into the money pit and escaped.

Nicky: changing your money story

Nicky grew up in the city. After finishing school, she spent a gap year in London—working a bit while she was there, but only earning enough to get by—and returned to Australia penniless. Nicky had committed to returning and completing her university degree. She joined the workforce soon after finishing university in a graduate role focused on human capital consulting. Her life continued at a fairly rapid pace: she married at 27 years of age, purchased a home and had brought twin girls into the world by the age of 30. Nicky's husband, Dave, had a steady business as a tradesman.

As a couple, they lived from pay cheque to pay cheque, bill to bill, mortgage repayment to mortgage repayment (mistake to mistake). Credit cards were used (more like abused, actually). Whenever they received an offer for a new credit card, they took it up. Most often they only made the minimum monthly repayment on the outstanding balance when the credit card statement arrived, incurring significant interest costs. They'd buy a new lounge or take a family holiday to Fiji 'on the card', and when they really wanted something new and the cards were maxed out, they would look at the 'Harvey Norman' deal. This is where you can pay nothing now, walk out of the store with the delivery booked and not pay anything for 24 months. Well, 24 months down the track, they suffered bill shock. Rather than scrambling to make the payment they would take the option of 'refinancing' and pay off the loan over another 24 months at a painful interest rate.

They weren't battlers, but they didn't save.

They were both very work driven. I mean, they loved working — or at least it seemed that way. I wondered if it was borne out of fear to stay ahead of their own spending, but it was more like they were so absorbed in their career trajectories (and career progression) and doing their jobs. Anything money related just sat in the backseat of their lives. You could say their financial literacy was stagnant.

Money wasn't on the agenda, nor were any money goals. By way of example, they went to a charity function with a group of friends, had a little too much to drink and with wild abandon committed $5000 to the auction — $5000 they didn't have! ('It was for a good cause and felt good and it seemed like everyone was doing it!') They dealt with the consequences later...ouch!

In their late 30s, the marriage broke down (this is often the time people get a wake-up call about their money mistakes). They went their separate ways. Each kept their super. They sold the house and repaid the bank with little to spare. Both faced that awful restart financially. They had been a train wreck from the beginning. Never once had they discussed financial goals or budgeted. They had cruised and managed, but it was always one foot in front of the other, maybe a few steps back. Yet one of the

(continued)

ongoing significant costs they were unable to escape in their divorce was their children's education.

They reached the decision to change their daughters' school for a whole host of reasons, financial strain being one of them. They always squabbled when the school fees arrived, arguing about who should pay. Neither of them was flush with cash — they had never budgeted for the school fees in the first place. They quickly learned about the cost pressures of paying rent for two homes (one each) with the kids going between them weekly.

Nicky had the drive to earn money but didn't have the focus to hang onto it.

For a period of time post-divorce, Nicky cut some of her outgoings but continued to live life, travelling overseas twice a year and paying off credit cards occasionally. She had a massive rent bill of $1000 per week and it just felt impossible to save towards buying a home again, especially in a suburb where she would like to live.

As Nicky was approaching her late 40s she had an 'aha' moment while reading the Sunday paper. There was a double page spread about the plight of homeless women and a couple of detailed stories on how these women had ended up without a home. The statistics showed that women over 55 were the fastest growing cohort of homelessness in Australia. There was also a story about a famous Australian (this is where it really hit home) who had ended up homeless. This drove home the 'aha' for Nicky. Nicky's own bias had her believing that this only happened to women with drug abuse issues. Her own financial security came into focus, and you could say it was the first time she had worried about money in the context of her lifestyle and getting older. Though it came a bit late, she realised this was one of those moments where she had to acknowledge her mistakes, own her money story and change it. Nicky would freely admit she had never budgeted in her life, let alone set a financial goal, but now was the time to start.

Can you see what has happened here? Nicky was the victim of her own income and expenses creep. Every day she was *borrowing from her future*, like so many of us learn to do.

The three biggest money mistakes

In my experience we tend to make three big money mistakes. Look at this list and ask yourself honestly, have you made any of these mistakes?

1. *Wearing and driving your money*. Do you always have a fancy car or the latest Louis Vuitton handbag, and dine at the hottest places in town wearing your most recent purchase?

   More than likely you buy things you don't need with money you don't have to impress people you probably don't even like!

2. *Doing nothing*. You have not paid any attention to money goals. You had considered doing something on occasion — which in no way constitutes a plan — but there was no planning, no goal setting…literally nothing. All the while, your superb income was devoured by no. 1. You have become what is known as a permanent wage slave.

3. No *understanding of baseline costs*. You don't know your 'open the front door' costs. You have never attempted to capture them, change them or reduce them.

Now, of course, there's always more to add insult to injury. For example:

- using multiple credit cards
- the Harvey Norman purchasing program
- relying on credit
- not paying off the monthly credit card balance'
- taking on costs such as expensive travel and school fees without the financial ability to pay for them.

What would you add to this list?

What are your top three money mistakes?

Take five minutes to write down your top three money mistakes.

1 _____

2 _____

3 _____

Now is the time to have a bit of fun. Call them out and share them with your partner, or call your sibling and remember that time when…

Sharing your mistakes out loud with someone is likely to encourage you to think again before making the same mistake.

Own up and own it

Making the decision to draw a firm line in your historical approach to money and commence shredding your lifetime of 'money baggage' is key to moving forward and rising from the pit.

Own those mistakes like your life and long-term financial security depend on it. Because you know they do!

The process that you need to undertake to successfully undo the mistakes is to review every expense you have incurred and decide where it needs to stop or continue. If you want to save money so you can be in a position to own a home by the time you retire (or to achieve some other meaningful financial goal) you need to start now. You might quickly realise now that retirement is likely much further away than you initially anticipated.

If you look back at Nicky's story, you'll see she had a goal. It might seem extreme to you reading that her goal was not to end up homeless. But what matters is that it gave her a reason to update her old money story, whereas previously she had no real reason to change her financial goals. Now she understands why she *must*.

Her new partner came along on this journey, and they combined their income power to buy a home. The house was nothing flash. It needed freshening up, but a foot in the door of the property market was a small relief for Nicky. They were savvy with their due diligence. It was important to obtain advice as they didn't have a lot of built-up knowledge or experience. (Note: *only invest in things you understand.*) They knew they would need to renovate, and this would be an additional cost they needed to allow for when re-establishing their baseline cost summary. Based on advice, they wanted to make sure that if they were indeed going to add to their investments later, they could readily rent the place out once renovated and earn a respectable yield, giving them optionality.

Fast forward another two years. With the equity in the house building (because of their principal and interest repayments), an improvement in house values in their area and an improved valuation from the bank due to their handy renovation work, they were able to borrow again, this time securing an investment property.

This involved a bit of a stretch, but this time Nicky's commitment to principal and interest payments would be aided by the rental income. This created a forced saving mechanism to help them both. To me, this is one of the greatest benefits of buying property: it creates a very powerful commitment from your income, and rather than the tail wagging the dog (that is, your lifestyle), the repayments go towards building an asset for you. There is no doubt it crimped their spending and created a clearer pathway for their retirement plans — and for their financial security too.

It doesn't matter what your age, getting in control of your spending and reigning it in can be a life saver.

Making choices and avoiding or owning up to your mistakes can deliver a level of financial independence that you didn't know you needed or knew was even possible. Nicky certainly didn't realise the significance of all her lost years, being a permanent wage slave heading into her late 40s, which would have otherwise seen no end and with nothing but great experiences to show for it (and a nice handbag or three).

Here are a few data points to help you own up:

♦ One in three first-time home buyers need five years to put together a deposit.

♦ The average deposit is 20 per cent of the value of the property.

♦ Credit card debt continues to rise.

♦ Homelessness is on the rise.

♦ In economically difficult times, the older you get, the more likely you are to lose your job.

Time to turn things around for you. Let's look at ways to assist you avoiding old money traps and repeating mistakes.

Assessing your income equation

It's time to talk income so that you can put some of your spending into perspective. I've purposefully held off talking about income until now because we tend to focus on that, and think we need more, but it's really our expenses that count.

You're aiming for your income to be greater, hopefully substantially greater, than your baseline costs determined in chapter 1. If that's not the case for you, you urgently need to cut your expenses and challenge yourself by owning your mistakes.

For the majority, this exercise can pose a great risk or a great opportunity. The great risk is that it might provide enough justification for you to continue on the expense creep treadmill. Instead, I'd like you to see this as an opportunity to identify *surplus* from which you can start to make better choices and build on your financial future.

Gather the information listed in the following table to confirm your income. For example, your net monthly pay, income from investment properties (net rent), dividends, other investment income or your business income (you should have an idea of how much this is based on your annual income tax return, if you're someone who pays tax quarterly). Capture all your income in this table.

Net monthly income sources	$
Net take-home pay	
Dividend and interest income	
Net rental income	
Business profit (net of tax estimate)	
Other	

(continued)

Net monthly income sources	$
Total net monthly income (X)	$
Total baseline costs (see chapter 1) (Y)	$
Income *surplus* (X – Y)	$
Baseline costs as a % of your income (Y/X)	%

Once you've determined your net monthly income, compare it with your baseline costs.

Ideally, your baseline costs won't exceed 75 per cent of your income. Here's a rule of thumb you can use as a guide to work towards:

- *baseline costs*
    - 50 per cent needs (food and shelter)
    - 25 per cent wants (holidays and lifestyle expenses)
- *savings*
    - 25 per cent savings from now on (or possibly expense creep in the past!)

This will help you plan directionally where your money goes and massively reduce money worries.

What if you're stuck in the pit with no escape?

If you realise that your baseline costs are far in excess of these ratios, you need to slash costs wherever possible. Consider everything that's discretionary and test it against the common money mistakes shared earlier.

Kick-start your refreshed approach to money now. After completing the exercises in chapters 1 and 2:

◆ commit to changes in your lifestyle to support your goals

◆ hold yourself accountable to your goals

◆ consider the expense ratios listed above to help guide you to a 'within your means' plan.

It might be helpful to know that, in Australia, the average percentage of income ratio dedicated to shelter (that is, rent or mortgage) is around 30 per cent, so planning to be in the range of 25 to 35 per cent is fair. What you might learn from looking at your income this way is that if you swing the pendulum too far one way or the other you may end up living beyond your means and unable to create a secure financial future.

Putting pressure on yourself by having rent or a mortgage repayment far greater than 30 per cent of your income will reduce your options now and down the track. An example of this might be that the pressure of paying these higher costs will restrict other life choices such as starting a business or changing your career. So, think ahead before overcommitting yourself. If you've got yourself into a money hole, keep revisiting the 'open your front door' costs. If those costs already represent a large chunk of your income as a percentage you might have to look at changing your house.

The interest rate climate also puts pressure on balancing expenses and needs to be taken into consideration. Give yourself a buffer, such as 5 per cent, to allow for increases in the cost of living. Ideally, using the percentage as a guide, you are creating flexibility with all your spending — within a framework — to help you.

In addition to the suggestions above, the average savings rate in Australia is just over 4 per cent. My view is that this is a result of expense creep — constantly chasing more and living beyond our means. My recommendation is to aim for a minimum of 25 per cent savings.

The consequence of the additional savings is, of course, less holidaying, clothing and entertainment. But before you moan, think about whether you are stealing from your future by spending on these things now.

As a quick, 10-minute activity to close off this chapter, can you identify any mistakes you may be making and how you can rectify them?

Coming to grips with your money mistakes

Grab a pen. You named your three biggest money mistakes earlier. Now think about other money mistakes you might be making. Write them in the table and consider what you can do to change them (for good). Name your solution (the action you need to take) for each and consider what the benefit will be to you. Why is this good for you and your future? (I've listed three examples in the table to get you started.)

Pain point	Solution	Benefit to you
I don't know my 'open my front door' costs	Review last month's credit card and bank statements	I will know where to start cutting costs and worry less about where my money is going
Monthly lease payment on car	Pay out remaining cost and buy a car I can afford	Monthly expense creep curtailed
Three credit cards in use	Reduce to one card and reduce credit card limit to within my means	I will be able to keep a closer eye on my expenditure and cap the risk of going off track with any one expense

Pain point	Solution	Benefit to you

What have you got to lose?

It's easy to look at someone else and think they are a financial mess — maybe they are and maybe they never had good role modelling, or maybe their money mistakes have them so deep in the poop they can't see a way out. Maybe they never discovered their 'why'. Maybe their parents were risk averse and were never prepared to take on debt of any kind.

Recognise that there's a way back from money mistakes. You can lose your 'money baggage' and come to grips with a new approach knowing your level of distress about your financial future can be reduced. Making a decision to live within your financial means and enjoy your lifestyle knowing that you also have the future covered is reason enough to find your way back.

A few changes can have a long-term positive impact on your physical, mental and economic health and financial security.

Stop worrying now

1. What are your biggest money pain points?

2. What costs have you unintentionally committed to that you need to address or cancel? Grab your diary and set aside some time to address each one. (I suggest one per day.)

3. Do you have a goal that gives you a significant reason to update your old money story? If so, what is it?

4. What do you need to change to help you consider a longer term approach to your financial future (and reconsider how you spend)?

Chapter 4
Build a trusted personal finance village

If there's one name that raises financial fear in the heart of every Australian (and is the topic of a fictitious TV series), it's Melissa Caddick.

It is alleged that the 49-year-old 'financial advisor' (I'll use that term loosely):

- created the persona of a successful businesswoman
- operated as an unlicensed financial advisor with fictitious qualifications
- fabricated share portfolio statements
- embezzled approximately $30 million from more than 70 clients, family and friends.

What we know for sure is that the façade continued for eight years. Caddick created an elaborate Ponzi scheme: a form of fraud that pays profits to earlier investors with funds from recent investors.

As a financial advisor, she was able to lure her friends and family in by demonstrating exceptional investment returns — on *paper*. Using the monies received from earlier investors, she produced detailed fake financial documentation to create the appearance of great returns being generated from their money. So, who wouldn't want in?

If someone needed to get out, she returned their earnings to them using a new investor's cash. All the while, Caddick lived it up using other people's money. To those who knew her, she created the illusion of a successful investment professional with expensive cars, clothes and holidays trips.

The story came to a crashing end after ASIC (the Australian Securities and Investments Commission) paid Caddick a visit at her home in 2020, after which she skipped town. ASIC was midway through an investigation at the time Caddick disappeared. The case was officially closed in 2021 when partial human remains were discovered on a beach and were confirmed to be Caddick's.

I vividly remember the interview on 60 *Minutes* with several of Caddick's clients. Most of them had tipped their only savings, including their hard-earned superannuation, into Caddick's hands.

Michelle Leslie was Caddick's personal trainer, turned close friend and investor. She was one of the victims of this charade. Caddick had tricked her into handing over her nest egg, money that she will never see again.

Cheryl and Faye, also friends of Caddick for more than 25 years, handed over $800 000 of their superannuation for Caddick to invest on their behalf. Also money never to be seen again.

In all, 72 investors became tangled up in Caddick's web of deceit. Everything Caddick had told them was a lie.

Unfortunately, in a lot of ways, you can see how this could easily happen to any one of us. Here's how it could go:

- We talk about what we're investing in with a family friend.

- The friend asks if we're interested in investing in something that is working well for them.

- We meet their 'financial advisor', who has all the relevant qualifications (all fake).

- The investment returns look good, or better than average.

- Other family or friends have already invested in it.

So why not just give it a go?

I'll tell you why. You need to do more than your fair share of due diligence when it comes to trusting people with your finances and investments, especially when there are links with family or friends.

When mixing family, friends and business goes bad

Time and time again, people have fallen into the trap of not doing their homework because they trusted the advice of a friend or a long-term mate, or most commonly a school or university friend.

Take, for example, James Packer (son of the late media mogul Kerry Packer) and Lachlan Murdoch (son of Rupert Murdoch, the British-Australian businessman and mass media heir). The sons of two of Australia's most successful media dynasties made their first large-scale foray into business life together, supposedly over a casual dinner one night. James mentioned to a few of his guests that 'a little mobile phone company' was doing good things profit-wise. Both entrepreneurs, James and Lachlan, went on to famously lose a share of their fortunes, totalling near on $1 billion, on the failed One.Tel at the height of the dot.com era.

In court, they said they had been 'profoundly misled as to the true financial position of the company' — which may have been true. It cost these young entrepreneurs dearly, not only in terms of financial wealth but also in terms of their reputations.

Although they both likely had quite a network of advisors at the time, I'll bet the one thing that James and Lachlan hadn't considered at the outset was the impact on their friendship, which still chews up headlines today.

I have seen this happen all too often, whether it's for $1 or $1 billion!

Why did they invest in the first place? The answer…a school friend! The leader of the pack was Jodee Rich, who belonged to an elite private school network that both James and Lachlan were a part of.

It can be a source of great tension and grief if things go bad financially between friends. Friendships may erode and the cascading impacts will be felt through your networks.

Investing with or being advised by friends or family is not a reason to cut corners on your due diligence.

So, who *can* you trust?

When you want to make an investment — a financial decision where you don't have to worry about your money — who can you go to so you don't get swindled?

Who do you trust?

I have a personal desire to ensure people have the best support when it comes to matters of money. And you really do need support. Don't be put off by Caddick's victims. Use their stories as a safeguard for what you can do differently. Work out a process that gives you comfort and peace of mind.

Some of the best advice in the business of finance (even if these sound like clichés) is:

◆ Never mix friends and financial advisors. If you do, have a third party to oversee everything.

- Don't develop a too personal relationship with your advisor. (Keep it on a professional level if you can.)

- If they're not transparent, walk away.

- If someone puts pressure on you to sign within a time frame, that's a red flag.

- Check the financial service's licence name.

Money and finances can be a highly emotional topic to discuss. It's complex because it's at the core of our livelihood. We might be very sensitive to the topic and not want to trust (or fall into the trap of trusting) family and friends when things are tough, or when we need to catch a break.

It's important to have a logical process and the right people around you. It can also be a good idea to have your accountant as a second person overseeing everything that your financial advisor recommends. (*Remember*: follow the same steps when selecting your accountant as you do for an advisor.)

A business colleague of mine has had a mixed run with money and seems to make the same mistakes all too often. He is 50 years old, paying rent, leasing a car and working month to month to support his family. He has been so preoccupied with business success that he neglected to get his personal financial house in order: not seeking advice when he should have, holding back because he felt he could sort out his finances himself. His trusted network is great for business, but he doesn't feel comfortable sharing the inner skeletons of his personal finance with them, so he doesn't. This causes him a lot of stress.

If you find yourself in this situation, recognise the gaps and weaknesses in your financial house and accept that you may need help to achieve the best financial outcomes for yourself.

You might feel emotional about it and need someone independent of you to help work through your particular situation.

Emotions often get in the way of good financial decisions and that's why you need a personal village of finance people who can help you get the best overall outcome.

We all need a little bit of help every now and then. Looking at your own financial future and your personal finance village is an important stepping stone to sound decision making.

Picking the right people for your personal finance village

The most successful businesses and families I have worked with have a network of trusted advisors and sounding boards that has been built over time. In the context of finances, I call this their personal finance village or PFV.

The old adage, 'It's not *what* you know, it's *who* you know' is the foundation to building your PFV made up of the right people. Your PFV should comprise trusted people who can help with money matters. When I say 'trusted', I mean people you have put through a filter — you need to do your due diligence. They must suit your unique needs (this is important). Your PFV should be different from anyone's else's PFV because your goals will be different from theirs.

Having qualified people around you is necessary to develop your financial literacy and set yourself up for success so you feel confident in the choices you make (and worry less) — and so you don't fall prey to the Caddicks of the world.

A PFV is something you should establish over time. You might seek someone for a specific reason only as a 'one-off'. Others may be required long term and, just like your GP, over time they will build up a long history with you. And sometimes, just as with a trusted GP, you may need to get a second opinion when the stakes are high.

I have, and have had, a range of people in my PFV. They have been sourced from my network and 'tested' by the network. They all have professional qualifications (I checked them out). Here's a snapshot of some more recent members of my village:

- *An accountant*: runs my business (yes, I have my own accountant!) even though I am an accountant. I value an 'outsider' looking in for me

- A *buyer's agent*: to help with the process of identifying the best locations to buy rental properties based on capital growth and rental yields and to also help scan the market more quickly than I could — somebody who is in the real estate game all day, every day

- A *business coach*: when transitioning from my executive career. While you might not see how this immediately relates to finance, a business coach will help you focus on and grow your business more quickly than anyone else can

- A *lawyer*: to review a contract for joining a board as a non-executive director. You might not have use for one now, but it's good to have someone on 'speed-dial' for when things come up that you haven't dealt with before. A good lawyer will also refer you to an alternative lawyer if it's not their specialisation.

Here are some other possibilities to assist you in addressing your money matters — and to assist you more broadly. Any one of these could be your trusted advisor.

Potential trusted advisor	How they might help
Financial advisor	Takes a bigger–picture view of your overall wealth and assists with making investment choices
Superannuation advisor	Could be the same person as your financial advisor
	Focused purely on the performance of your personal superannuation (usually this would apply when you have a self-managed super fund)
Stockbroker	Main function is to identify when stocks on the share market are bought and sold, preferably for a profit!
Estate planning lawyer	Specialist in their field and best used for preparing and reviewing your will
Bookkeeper	Records your cash flow in and out and prepares your BAS (business activity statement)
Private banker	Usually accessible if you have a certain level of debt or assets. Acts as a good advocate for you at the bank when borrowing money or requiring help with bank products for savings or investments
Tax agent	Prepares and lodges your income tax returns on time
Tax advisor	For technical issues such as how best to structure yourself into an asset or business; may help on all manner of issues (capital gains tax, loans etc.)
Psychologist	To talk about 'money baggage'; some of this comes from relationships and family history (it can be good to talk these things through with a psychologist)
Personal coach	If you're looking for motivation or direction, this is a great place to start
Insurance broker	It's handy to have someone you can call on for advice on life, TPD, trauma and income protection insurances. Also, if something goes wrong, they can assist with the process of rectifying it

We all need good, diverse people around for guidance with our personal finances. You won't need all of these people at all stages of your life, so it's worthwhile considering who is currently in your village, who you might need to add and who might need to be removed, depending on your current money goals.

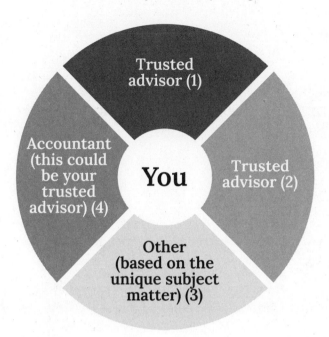

Who's in your village?

Take 10 minutes to reflect on your village: who do you need and where are your skill gaps?

Make an action plan to kick off your research for that one addition to your village or at least 'fact check' the ones you currently have.

My personal finance village

Trusted advisor (1)

Trusted advisor (2)

I'd like to share a story that will highlight for you the importance of choosing the right people for your PFV.

Mel and Kim: how to know who you need and when — a cautionary tale

Some time ago I was introduced to a couple, Mel and Kim. Kim's family had a retail business that was ticking along successfully and always provided a good level of income for the family. Kim did not work in the family business. Mel, however, worked alongside Kim's father. For 20 years they had used the same accountant and business advisor, Peter.

Peter had always worked directly with Kim's father and occasionally with Mel on matters relating to the day-to-day operations of the family business. Kim had only recently engaged Peter for her own money matters as he was the only accountant she knew and as she had known him for a long time it made sense. This is where it gets interesting.

Kim had built a very successful career for herself (outside the family business). She had accepted a senior role in a corporate organisation and was offered shares and options in the company. It took some time for Kim to seek advice from Peter about the shares. Kim needed to know what the tax implications of these shares and options would be, now and in the future. Peter had always been focused on the family business, and particularly on Kim's father, and it turned out Peter was not well qualified in shares and options and perhaps didn't consider the significance of Kim's shares. The dollar value of the shares and options at the time Kim first raised them with Peter may not have seemed significant. However, this quickly changed, and while Peter became aware of their increase in value his actions didn't reflect this.

Luckily for Kim, it was at this point that her suspicions of Peter's 'lack of interest' and perhaps lack of technical knowledge led her to look further. She contacted her banker, who gave her the name of a qualified professional to talk to about her shares and options. This introduction proved to be crucial for Mel and Kim as the value of the shares and options grew considerably to become worth many times their combined annual incomes.

Nevertheless, the delay in seeking advice from a qualified professional cost Mel and Kim a net of $6 million in taxes, due to the capital gains cost of selling shares. But the damage would have been $8 million because they saved $2 million by getting the right advice in the end.

Sadly, getting the right advice identified that Peter had already made fatal errors to the tune of $9 million. These errors could not be fixed retrospectively and had already cost Kim and Mel dearly.

The family was loyal to Peter (which is a common story). He was good as an advisor to the family business because he had a detailed knowledge of it. The business had a retail focus, which was Peter's specialty.

On the other hand, he was not across executive share option matters in the level of detail needed to ensure Mel and Kim benefited from the upside and minimised tax wherever possible to improve their overall outcome. This was no small matter — in fact, the success of these shares was life changing for Mel and Kim. The sale of Kim's shares provided long-term financial security that may never have been possible from the intergenerational retail business.

Here are the main factors that played a part in Mel and Kim's awful tax bill:

1. the delay in getting the right advice upfront
2. recognising that while Peter was great at working for the family business, he did not have the experience to deal with shares
3. not seeking another opinion quickly

4. trusting their gut that Peter's strengths were not in options and shares

5. Peter not acknowledging quickly that he was out of his depth.

As you can see, there could be $2 million worth of reasons why it's critical to have the right people around you for your particular situation or scenario.

> ### *Don't just stick to what you know, who you know or to continuing to do things the same way.*

How to handle a new financial challenge

So, let's take Kim's story a bit further. Let's assume there was no existing relationship with an advisor — that is, there's no Peter.

You are now in Kim's shoes. What is the best way for Kim to decide who to trust with managing her shares and options for the best possible tax outcome?

Here are 10 steps you can apply to a new financial challenge like owning shares and options when determining the best way to approach it and how to seek the best support:

1. *Educate yourself.* Ensure you understand the shares and options you are being offered by the company.

2. *Recognise your skill gap.* See the significance of the shares and options as a 'trigger'. By trigger, I mean do something different — change it up. Ask yourself, *Who do I need to add to my PFV to get this right?*

3. *Ask your advisor for a referral.* Ask your bank manager if they know anyone who could advise you. (In truth, this is what saved Kim, because they introduced Kim to a qualified advisor.)

4. *Check in with your internal network.* Ask someone at your company (perhaps another employee) if there is someone they worked with previously when offering these shares/options.

5. *Seek confirmation that they are appropriately qualified.* Meet with the recommended person or people to ask, 'Do you have the right skills to advise me?' Or 'Have you dealt with this type of situation before?'

6. Ask, *'How much will it cost?'* Ask about the cost or fee for the advice. How would they structure their cost or fee?

7. *Build trust.* It takes time and this will be a good opportunity for you to get to know this advisor.

8. *Do your due diligence.* Ask to speak to some existing clients of this new advisor to help build a greater understanding of their experience and what has worked well for them.

9. *Check that their professional qualifications are suitable.* The greatest risk we all face is using unqualified people. There are plenty of scammers out there who fake professional qualifications. There are also professionals with huge egos who are too big to say, 'I think you need someone else to look at this'.

10. Admit *'you're not right for me'.* All too often we feel an obligation to continue when we need to *stop*. At the end of the day, the buck stops with you so if you aren't feeling it, you need to terminate this business or personal relationship (so far as it relates to this matter). I know you have invested time and energy into getting to know this advisor (and the thought of doing this all over again with someone new is painful or downright annoying), but you may need to start afresh.

Seek first to understand what you are contemplating before you seek out advice.

If Kim had followed more of these steps sooner, in addition to the $2 million saved, she could have saved an additional $9 million that was missed due to Peter's earlier error. That's one very expensive lesson! Thank goodness she (eventually) followed her instinct.

Fact-check your finance village

If you went back and interviewed Caddick's 72 victims, you would find that they all wished they had checked more of the details, such as the professional qualifications that Caddick purported to hold, including a financial services licence.

It was only when ASIC contacted some of them that they started to dig deeper — for example, by calling CommSec (the Commonwealth Bank of Australia's share trading platform) to confirm their account details, only to find no such account existed.

Fact checking is at odds with how we generally respect professionals but if there is one key takeaway from all of these stories it is that, regardless of how 'well' we know — or a friend knows — the advisor, we must do our fact checking.

Here's a checklist of key criteria to assist you with building your village. (Note: your first point of call may be to go to the professional association to ask for someone experienced who can help you, then confirm they have the right skills.)

Skills and qualifications checked

☐   Known by someone you trust

☐   Demonstrates experience with your circumstance or issue

☐   Track record with solving issues like yours

☐   You have a good rapport

☐   Your gut responds well to this person

- [ ] If you are seeking a family member's opinion, confirm they are qualified to advise you on this matter (they may give you a better emotional radar than a financial one, which is also important)

- [ ] Ensure you fully understand the issue that you are seeking advice on

In short:

Beware the huge ego

Beware the smooth talker

Beware the salesperson

Beware the name dropper (pet dislike of mine)

Beware the friend of a friend...

Fess up when things go wrong!

A friend recently shared a story about a husband and wife who lived in a well-to-do suburb in a capital city. The wife was always out shopping, getting facials, playing tennis, and so on. She used a credit card to pay for everything and there had never been any issues with it. So she was shocked when her husband's business went south and they had to sell their beautiful, prestigious house to pay off the debts and to consider renting. Her husband was too proud, or too embarrassed, to admit that the business was failing and continued without advice or support only to find the hole he had dug was so deep there was no way out.

I have a bank of these kinds of stories relating to people and issues with money. The hardest conversation to have with a client is where they went wrong on an issue when they didn't get prior advice.

My advice here is simple. Don't be afraid to come clean if you're in a mess. Advisors are usually in the business to help and it's better to come clean now than wait because things can fester and get much worse.

It's too late when you've sold your business to minimise tax. It's too late when you've purchased shares in your name instead of, say, a trust. It's too late if you didn't save for your tax bill. It's too late when you have already signed the contract!...Some things can be amended or adjusted but the best outcomes are the considered ones.

Just remember that, first and foremost, you need to be in control of your finances.

A final friendly piece of advice

Our friends can be an incredible source of knowledge and wisdom, in most cases. Friends do have a valid part to play in your finances. But it is just that: they may play a *part*. The worst thing you can do is stick your head in the sand and ignore everything or everyone around you. I also caution you on opinion shopping. Don't drop the ball on your own due diligence. Continue to do your research and fact checking regardless of the source.

I like the story of former professional basketballer Shaquille O'Neal, who has an entourage of business and financial advisors, but found he was turning up to meetings and being treated like the 'sports jock'. It drove him crazy because people would pitch their business ideas to his team and virtually ignore him. He decided to take matters into his own hands and went and got an MBA (Master of Business Administration) so that he could be in charge.

That's exactly what you need to do: be in charge of your finances.

Stop worrying now

1. Considering your current money matters and looking to the future, what issues give rise to a worry or worries that you could resolve now by talking to someone new (who will join your PFV)?

2. Take a moment to reflect on your current PFV: the connections, relationships and level of trust you have established. What do you need to do now to strengthen the ones you have? What probing questions can you ask them that will help cement these professional relationships?

3. Having considered where the gaps might be in your own PFV, if you are working with an advisor now who isn't the right fit, what steps will you take to change that relationship and move on?

4. Take action to connect, book a cuppa with and get to know someone you need to add to your PFV. What outcome would you like to achieve from working with them?

Chapter 5
Aim to be financially free-er

I'm sure, like me, you've read the news headline 'How to be financially free' more than once. Did it make you want to run and hide? Does the expectation that you would like to be financially free contribute to your stress and anxiety about your money and position in life? Because, let's face it, for most of us, jetting off into the sunset on a private plane probably feels like a long way off from where we currently are.

Financial freedom is not a thing or a place where you might land. Rather, think of it as an ethos, a way of life! It's a process I'm going to teach you through this book: knowing what is truly important, knowing what your real cost of living is and learning about how to be guided by your true north, as well as living your life aligned to your goals, including your financial goals.

My issue with the term 'financial freedom', and the reason why I believe it contributes to stress, is because it feels like a destination, one that most of us think we'll never get to.

Financial freedom could be defined in a number of different ways:

- being debt free

- living within your means (understanding the trap of income and expense creep)

- having a dependable income and feeling in control of your finances

- having enough passive income not to have to work for a long time, or possibly ever again

- having enough cash, savings and investments on hand to afford the lifestyle that you desire

- having the monetary stability to do what you want in life without having to worry about your bank account

- having enough financial resources to pay for your living expenses and to allow you to afford your life goals.

Stop and think. What does it mean to *you* to be financially free?

The truth is, most people think the answer to financial freedom is to have a bit — no, a lot — more money than they currently have (even if they're ridiculously wealthy). A nest egg or a pot of gold somewhere that means they will never have to worry about money again. Isn't this the stuff dreams are made of? Mmm, where do we find that? (*Side note*: if you don't set your money goals you'll never get there.)

But just how much is 'enough' for us to feel financially free?

Would $100 000 be enough? What about $1 million or maybe $10 million?

Human behaviour would suggest no amount is enough if you don't have a very clear plan for what exactly freedom is for you. What is important to you? What are your priorities?

It is not how much you have, but the choices you make with what you have, that will lead you to financial freedom.

Beware the 'have more, want more' trap

Joshua Becker, in his book *Things that matter most*, states, 'Does accumulating lots of money and possessions offer a pathway to a state of happiness? Culture says yes. Science says no'. We all think we need more money than we do. Why?

I am often reminded by one of my sons that we live in a capitalist world. He's lucky to be wise (at 22 years of age). He lives reasonably frugally, and definitely subscribes to the 'minimalist' approach in all aspects of life. He purchases good-quality second-hand clothing (many vintage items), sells what he no longer needs online and shops once a week to a budget (and doesn't waste food). He is strategic with his 'birthday wishes' and God forbid you buy him an ornament...expect that to end up in the bin. He recognises the traps of our capitalist world, such as every Apple launch pitching the latest and greatest new device that we 'must have' and the expectations to travel the world to Instagrammable destinations. And...you guessed it...he worries about money.

Your Instagram feed, the billboards you see as you drive down the road, magazines, the radio, podcasts...everyone, everywhere is trying to sell you on why buying this 'thing' is more important than anything else when it comes to your money. It's easy to feel trapped (actually surrounded) by it. Each new advertisement encouraging us to buy more, more, more stuff—one example being click frenzies such as Black Fridays that plague our in 'spam' boxes. It's likely this only adds to your money worries.

The more 'stuff' you buy, the more money you then need.

But a lot of this stuff doesn't actually make us happy.

Have you ever been in the position where you felt you could splash out, maybe using a Christmas bonus? So you take a nice holiday, spend a bit more on the family over the break and then discover, come February when the bills start to arrive, that not only has the bonus evaporated, but you've also spent twice the amount you received. So now, you're right back where you started: enduring credit card debt and several disciplined months to get back on track.

On and on we go, earning more, spending more.

The more we earn, the more we buy or spend.

The more we buy, the more we want...

We keep moving the goalpost of what we need to earn to feel free and happy...but it's a vicious cycle because then we earn more and we spend more buying this stuff...Each time you are drawn into the spending vortex, your goal of 'being financially free' keeps moving further and further away. When does this cycle ever actually end?

But rich people have enough, right?

You may think, *surely there must be a level of wealth at which I would be financially free. What about the super-rich — they're financially free, aren't they?*

The University of Queensland used data from the World Values Survey — a large-scale global survey covering 150 000 participants from 78 countries — to examine the relationship between social class and the desire for wealth and status. They found that the upper class yearn for more wealth and status, indicating the 'have more, want more' phenomenon. Statistically, this means the more you earn, the more likely it is you will yearn for more. According to the authors of the research, the rich want more because their wealth and status are essentially linked to their identity.

Whether your level of wealth is a lot or a little, this is a mindset trap. My view is you will not achieve financial freedom unless you get there via the disciplined, even boring, path of aligning your values and your essential cost base (making the changes that will be needed), and thinking about how you spend (or don't spend) to create freedom — not an ever-increasing and never-ending cost base. It's important to realise that financial freedom is not an idyllic destination that you will magically arrive at one day.

Financial freedom is an open bucket and the best way to address this is by linking your priorities and monetary goals to your vision for freedom.

To be free we need to set realistic money goals, and determining those goals may give you greater clarity on what freedom means or what it looks like for you. There are plenty of options for creating a life that's free of money worries, but they require effort and in many cases accountability by you!

Does that mean you need to sign up to a life of frugality and live like a monk?

Well, that's up to you — depending on what you value *and* what you truly need to be financially *free-er*.

You may choose to consciously save, consistently invest, avoid spending a lot of money, avoid unnecessary waste, declutter and recycle. But the scale at which you do that can vary.

Realising that money isn't everything is the most important measure of having enough money.

When is enough money actually *enough*?

The truth is there's no magic number. There are people who are objectively well off but can't see the forest for the trees, and others who don't earn much at all but are in a fantastic financial position: happy and worry-free.

Plenty of people who prioritise money over their personal relationships or morals live to regret their wealth and destroy their close relationships (I've seen this time and time again!). To be truly rich and grounded is to have great relationships with your family and friends and to be proud of your achievements.

So it's important to know what to value and invest in, and keep on top of your goals.

Let me explain, using Roger as an example.

Roger: how much is enough?

He was on the precipice of creating his own financial freedom, being set for life (by his definition) and actually having *enough*—finally! He knew that with the successful sale of his business he wouldn't have to worry about money any more and he wouldn't have to work so hard in the future. But then it all went horribly wrong...

Roger sold his business and pocketed about $10 million. (How nice is that! Wouldn't you love a cool $10 million to set you up for life?)

The fatal mistake Roger made was that at the time he sold he didn't consult his 'village' or draw up a plan to ensure that his financial freedom would remain intact. In fact, fairly quickly he paid off his mortgage and upgraded his home ($3.5 million), bought a beach house ($2 million), helped out some of his family

($1 million), took a year off, bought furniture and cars, put a bit into his super and paid his tax (circa $3+ million)...with a bit left over as a cash buffer.

The extra annual cost to upkeep the bigger family home, the holiday house and meeting the increased financial family expectations was well over $100 000 per year. It would never be enough. Within a short space of time, he was back in a full-time job working for a boss.

Now, 10 years later, he's still working and possibly none the wiser as to what happened. Still dreaming about financial freedom and still worrying about money. So, in this case, a $10 million windfall wasn't really 'enough' because it disappeared just like that!

Roger was a victim of his own success — income and expense creep on steroids. He had no plan and in the blink of an eye his financial freedom was frittered away. He no doubt thought he had arrived on the island of financial freedom, but it was a mirage. That's why I think about financial freedom as a journey, an ethos, a way of life.

Instead of striving for financial freedom, the destination, your time and energy are best directed to getting on the journey and not worrying about the destination.

Financial freedom as a way of life (not a destination)

It's all about having the freedom to make choices about how and where you work (for how much and how long) and how you live your life. This comes in many forms and it's where you take control of your money story to create a version of freedom that works for you.

The journey to financial freedom could look like this for you:

- fewer money worries; less stress, pressure and anxiety

- flexibility to work anywhere as much or as little as you like

- no longer just a 'cog in the wheel' in some company where you are an employee

- getting your life back

- possibly working three rather than five days a week

- doing more of what you love

- building capital and living on the income it creates

- considered lifestyle choices, e.g. local vs overseas holidays, electric vs petrol vehicles

- more time with family

- more time for your hobbies, playing sport...whatever you choose.

Here's how that looks in reality.

Mandy and Scott: trapped on the financial treadmill of life

Clients of mine, Mandy and Scott — a power couple — had good jobs, were entitled to healthy bonuses, had regular pay rises and were pretty comfortable with life. But they were loaded with credit card debt from their upmarket lifestyle. Call them perfect victims of income and expense creep who were absolutely trapped on the financial treadmill of life and, if I'm honest, suffering terribly from other people's expectations of them.

They lived in an affluent suburb where it seemed everyone knew who was who. Their cars were leased, they paid private school fees, had expensive holidays and lovely jewellery — they basically had everything they could want. They decided they needed help

> to put together a plan that wouldn't completely compromise their current world but would move them towards a future with far greater freedom. In this case, freedom from needing to constantly earn a big salary and from being slaves to their own expense creep.

So how did Mandy and Scott stop the treadmill and start planning to secure their financial future?

Let's walk through the six steps Mandy and Scott considered to build their financial future and give themselves the freedom they were looking for.

You'll be familiar with these steps from having completed the exercises in earlier chapters so I'll keep the points big picture here. Use them to help you determine how to action your own plan.

1. Determine your baseline costs

We covered this in chapter 1 when we talked about recognising your income and expense creep, and then confirming your 'open your front door' costs, followed by developing your new (and honest) baseline cost summary. This was a very powerful exercise for Mandy and Scott as they quickly discovered they could reduce some of their expenses by planning ahead (being a little less frivolous) and not splashing out unnecessarily. I know it frightened them a little bit too, seeing how easily they spent their money without considering the consequences. They realised taking more time to understand the outgoings freed up income that could be invested and helped reduce their reliance on their income every month.

2. Set meaningful goals

Following a clear and truthful baseline analysis enables breathing space to consider your goals. For Mandy and Scott, this meant realising that greater consideration of their outgoings allowed them to think more about their future goal. Their meaningful goal was to not be so reliant on both of them being in highly stressful executive roles *forever*! Once they set their goal, it came to life. They could direct so much more energy and time to making it a reality. Agreeing on their goal was incredibly powerful. It was like a giant filter over their spending and helped them create the capacity they needed (by spending less) to save for their future.

3. Identify obvious ways to reduce costs and create savings

It's likely that at this step you'll discover that, like Mandy and Scott, you want to reign in some lifestyle costs. For example, if you don't pay off the full balance on every credit card every single month, you should start making this a habit. If you lease your car, don't. Buy a car you can afford to pay for. While a lease or a credit card may seem like a good idea at the time, they ultimately add a significant financial burden to your monthly expenses.

Here are some of the best savings tips you can *immediately* look at actioning:

- Start saving 20 per cent of your income and automate it: make it a habit by setting up an automatic bank transfer to another bank account that you have set aside (preferably with a better interest rate than your day-to-day one). *Note:* If you want financial independence sooner, set aside more than 20 per cent.

- And why stop at 20 per cent? Take your savings a step further. Once you have confirmed your 'open the front door' costs and you're clear on your essential baseline costs, commit to saving the rest of your income.

- Stop unnecessary spending by cancelling the endless subscriptions.

- Eat in, and take away less. Both your wallet and waistline will thank you for it. We all know cooking at home can save you bucketloads.

- Get out of debt: focus on reducing your debt as quickly as possible.

- Make extra payments on your mortgage.

- Avoid carrying around credit cards if you're a spendthrift (and in any case, pay them off first).

4. Enable your personal finance village

Get help to identify where you may have some surplus cash or income and plan to capture it before it gets spent. Your village is critical here, especially if you are starting afresh. Equally, having a trusted advisor tell you straight out, for example, that you aren't living within your means might be just what you need to focus on your goals.

Getting the village working with and around you will support easier decision making. It's times like this when you might be too emotionally connected or attached to your lifestyle and can't see the wood for the trees, so having someone independent test your views or put the mirror up will go a long way to helping you make choices with a future focus. Also, when considering the members of your village, try not to have just one financial advisor to blindly follow (remember Melissa Caddick), but a trusted (small) number of people to help you plan and execute on a strategy towards greater financial freedom — which we talked through in chapter 4.

To get you started, sit down with your accountant or other trusted advisor. If you have a partner, engage them in this too. Begin with the end in mind. With your income and existing baseline costs on hand, ask what steps you can take or what suggestions they have to create a path for you to become debt free. (Or you could ask a question that's aligned to you feeling financially free-er.)

5. Design your dream life

When you stop for a moment, it's amazing how simple your vision of the 'dream life' can actually be. What is your vision five to 10 years from now? How would you like to reflect on it? We will cover this in more detail in chapter 10, but here's something to consider at this design phase.

If freedom to you is leaving your big-salary job (or stepping off the treadmill), you'll need to consider over what period of time to adjust or lower your baseline costs and many other items connected with your salary. It's easy to assume you might earn less. This might be true initially, but you could replace that income with running your own business, or adding another dimension to your design. So, once you're clear what your dream life looks like, you can scrutinise every cost (and your income) against this and decide if it gets you closer.

6. Invest to secure your financial freedom

We all need to save and invest *more*. Over a period of days, weeks, months and years all these decisions will add up. You need to consider both passive (interest income, rental income, dividends) and active assets (businesses, including share trading) as a way to create wealth to help with securing your financial future. You need to make conscious decisions about every dollar that comes in and before it goes out. Choose assets that will grow rather than committing to future liabilities such as overspending on credit cards, entering a lease to buy a new car or falling into the Harvey Norman (aka buy-now-pay-later) cycle.

Wealth accumulation, in the main, is a long, slow and conscious process. You need to be deliberate with the money you earn, how you earn it, the way you plan to invest it, how you take on debt or pay down debt and how you add to your superannuation or create other investment opportunities. We've spent plenty of time getting your baseline costs in order and developing a vision for your financial future (and your version of freedom).

Let's now look at ways you can invest. These may include savings (using term deposits and high-interest accounts), comparing renting versus buying, investment properties, buying or building a business, buying shares and crypto.

TERM DEPOSIT OR SAVINGS ACCOUNT

Putting your money into a term deposit is certainly better than it sitting in a bank account with a close-to-zero interest rate. Most banks offer special rates when you contribute more regular deposits to your bank account or a high-interest bank account that benefits your savings strategy overall — and is the start of a new stream of passive income for you.

PROPERTY

Renting versus buying: consider the differences for you. Different life stages influence this significantly, but it's good to know how each option works for your money. Renting is a popular strategy because you have no stamp duty, the landlord picks up some of the bills and you have greater flexibility with where you live. The downside may be that you don't access capital growth and you are at the mercy of a landlord. Buying a home may reduce your financial stress when you are getting closer to retirement. Many people see this as part of their nest egg: you can sell up, downsize and live off the proceeds.

Buying an investment property, as opposed to a home, will also set you on a path to financial independence. If you are a wage earner, the banks are more likely to lend you money if you want to buy a residential or investment property than if you showed up wanting to borrow to buy shares in a public company or for a share of a business. The trick here is to find the right balance between how much you must borrow or can borrow, the costs of maintaining the property (all the outgoings) and the rent (the income you receive),

Like all investments, regardless of who you seek advice from, it's good to do your homework. When looking at an investment property (and before you buy), here are a few things to consider:

◆ *Spend time at the site (the house, unit or business premises).* This will help you get a feel for the type of traffic (meaning cars or people) that goes by, the position of the property (e.g. everyone raves about north-facing properties for natural light).

- *Consider the age and the state of repair of the property.* This will give you an indication of how soon you might be up for some expensive renovations or replacements — think, blinds/windows (if timber), carpets/floor coverings, dishwasher, oven, heating and air conditioners, condition of the paint (is it peeling off?).

- *Get a pest and building report.* Getting this checked out by a qualified person is a must. Be sure you read it thoroughly and investigate any issues that concern you.

- *Obtain a strata report (if you're looking at something in a block of flats/units/apartments).* Review all the minutes, look at the balance in the sinking fund and understand any capital works that have been undertaken.

- *Shop around for insurance.* There are lots of different types of insurance that you need to consider, such as landlords insurance, building insurance and contents insurance.

- *Get an independent valuation.* Seek this from a registered valuer *before you buy.* Having the property valued independently will reduce the risk of you overpaying for a property you really 'want' and will help you get clear on the true condition of the property and price comparatives for similar properties in the same market.

BUYING OR BUILDING A BUSINESS

You might be considering buying or building a business as an investment or as part of your future plans to create a new or additional income stream. You might want to try something new or kick off your dream to be your own boss. There is a tonne of things to consider if you are going to *buy* an existing business or *build* a new business and I'll cover this in greater detail in chapter 11.

Please consider the following in conjunction with advice *before* entering into a new or existing business:

- Do you have any previous experience with this type of business?

- Do you have any industry knowledge?

- Do you know anyone in this industry?

- Do you understand the cash flows of this business?

- Make sure you understand if the cash flows are consistent, sporadic or seasonal.

- Review the financial statements and the tax returns for the last three years.

- Be aware of any existing contracts or customers.

- Get to know the existing team.

- Have you visited the business premises (this can be very important if you're considering a franchise — again, look at the people, traffic, etc.)?

- What are the trade-offs for you?

SHARES

Many of us indirectly own shares already via our super funds and possibly play a non-active role in investing this way.

Building a share portfolio takes time and research and may not be for you. Consider the steps above before investing in the share market because you will effectively be investing in someone else's business. Shares can be a great source of income as they generally produce a dividend income and, if chosen well, may grow in value. There is plenty of advice online and you can easily sign up to one of the share services provided by the banks or other platforms and trade shares for a base fee. The same rules apply as above. In addition, consider:

- Do you have experience with this?

- What research have you done?

- Do you need to add someone to your personal finance village to help with this?

- Are you making this investment decision because someone else said it was a good idea?

CRYPTOCURRENCY

For the uninitiated, cryptocurrency (or 'crypto') is a newer form of investment. Crypto is a digital currency, so it's not the same as cash or shares but similar in the way that you use it to buy other digital assets. Instead of your cash sitting in the bank, crypto sits in your crypto wallet. It goes by many names, including Bitcoin (which Blockchain technology was invented for) and Ethereum. It is also not regulated in the same way as banking or the share markets are, so you need to keep this in mind when considering crypto as an investment because it's high risk. The investment you are buying with your crypto is not a physical thing; it is electronic and includes digital assets such as non-fungible tokens (NFTs) for ownership of something unique like a piece of art, collectibles or even a tweet! Proceed with caution and do your due diligence.

How to deal with a windfall

Consider this. A small number of you will be fortunate enough to experience receiving a lump sum of cash at some point. It's unlikely to be something you planned for, and more likely to be totally unexpected.

It could come in the form of:

- a family member dying and leaving you some money (inheritance)
- a lotto win (well done!) 😊
- marrying into a family with money (which could be a curse)
- selling a rare piece of memorabilia that you own for a large sum of money after a musician or sportsman has passed away.

Other windfalls might include the following:

- a capital gain for the sale of a significant asset, such as your home or shares you have owned for a long time
- being granted employee share options

- sale of your house for a lot more than you paid for it

- a juicy redundancy payment

- a new job or promotion and a new title with a much bigger pay packet

- a healthy sign-on bonus

- sale of a business that you have been building for a short or long time.

You will need to take time to consider re-adjusting your financial goals accordingly if you are in receipt of a windfall gain and deciding how to use the money wisely. Don't blow it all at once!

Remember Roger in our earlier story? Rather than investing the money from his business sale in the beach house costing $2 million (lifestyle asset) with an ongoing financial cost (land tax, rates, maintenance, electricity, internet etc.), had he invested the same amount in assets that produced, say, a 7 per cent return, he would have created a forever income stream of $140 000 per year. Instead, he had an annual cost of well over $25 000 just to keep it. That's a sizeable difference. The only income *dependence* is on Roger to keep working to maintain the property rather than enjoying other pursuits while earning investment income.

Reassess your goals now that you have more money to work with: don't be a sucker for a new business venture, a few more expensive toys or an extravagant home.

There may be some unwanted side effects of winning due to rash decisions, which seem to follow the moment people hear about their windfall. You're in a wealth honeymoon right now and your judgement may be blurred. Someone might try to take advantage of your newfound wealth, you are at greater risk of being scammed or robbed or you may now be in the spotlight after enjoying relative anonymity. Greater complexity will no doubt initially weigh you down and increase your money worries.

Hit the pause button, take a deep breath and head back to the beginning of the book before making any rash decisions.

'Get rich quick': if it sounds too good to be true, it is

Ever heard of Elizabeth Holmes? She founded a company called Theranos, which was a blood-testing technology start-up once valued at $9 billion, until its epic fall from grace after allegations came to light that its technology was a fraud.

The then CEO, Elizabeth, and the company president, Ramesh, made claims that were never demonstrated and that amounted to outright deceit. It made headlines and was so newsworthy that John Delves wrote an award-winning book called *Bad blood: secrets and lies in a Silicon Valley startup*, which is also the subject of a TV adaptation, *The dropout*. Many famous investors were totally blind-sided — to the tune of US $700 million!

So what's in this story for you?

Be realistic about the investment you are putting your hard-earned cash into. Ask yourself: *Could I spare the cash if I were to never see it again?*

Beware the headlines or the chat around the BBQ about the latest and greatest company. Has anyone ever suggested to you to 'put it all on black' or to put your money on Race 5 at Randwick? These are the seeds or moments when the little devil called 'getting rich quick' tickles you. Don't fall for it. The quick win may be short-lived. It's easy to fall into the trap of a long-term friend or partner seeking your contribution to their new business. Doing your due diligence is the best way to protect your money.

Your financial freedom and security will be a direct result of choices you make over a long period of time, not a short one.

Don't wait until it's too late

Some time ago, I sat down with a colleague who was transitioning from a CEO role. He was busily going from meeting to meeting, catching up with business colleagues (past and present). He was being offered new CEO and board roles, and new business ventures to take a stake in. It was quite tortuous riding the high of a successful tenure as CEO and balancing up all the possibilities of what to do next. This wasn't about earning more money as he was already financially independent and felt secure, but the pull to do more was strong.

He was flat out working through his next big thing when he received two phone calls close together. One call was from his best friend to tell him her super-fit husband had had a heart attack (and was on life support) and the other was from a close friend who had been diagnosed with terminal cancer and had only a few months to live. My colleague stopped searching right there, considered his options, and decided he needed to enjoy life, slow down a little, spend more time with his family and travel more.

Having financial choices was at the core of this adjustment to his path to financial freedom. He decided enough was enough. In this case, experiencing life trumped more slog.

Sometimes a health scare or some bad news can have you rethinking your financial goals and adjusting what financial freedom looks like for you going forward. Equally, it might be just the wakeup call you need.

Ultimately, don't leave it until it's too late because the key to creating financial freedom is time.

Stop worrying now

1. Jot down your vision for financial freedom.

2. Make a decision on three steps you are going to take today towards developing your path to financial freedom. For example, setting up a new bank account for your *new* savings; opening a share trade account; ditching the money baggage of... [insert whatever your money baggage is].

3. Consider this scenario (my personal favourite): you come home to discover that a distant relative has left you a substantial sum of money. After some champagne (naturally!), you realise you can pay off your mortgage — in fact, you can pay all your bills. So you decide to take three months off work. What else would you do?

Chapter 6
Plan for your death (seriously!)

What happens to your money when you die?

That question is usually enough to make you cringe, groan, change the subject or turn the page — *don't!*

The subject of dying or death is an awkward one. It is made even more difficult by topics such as money or wealth, especially if you aren't used to talking about those either!

I've spent most of my career asking people if they've given death some thought and it elicits all kinds of responses, usually 'it can wait' or 'we'll get to it later'. Then there are the immortals, the ones who say, 'Oh that's not going to happen!' (*Spoiler alert*: it is at some point, and often by surprise!)

In many respects, I admire the idea of living life without the thought that it might end. But we can't live forever, like Dracula. Yet we just can't stand to spend any time thinking about life without ourselves in it! We don't give the subject of death any airplay, and we shut down any conversations about the potential end or our demise on this planet.

Worse still, most people contemplate their Will when they have had a bad health diagnosis or a brush with death.

For example, I was working with a gentleman who knew he was unwell; he'd been told by his doctor that he would die from his illness. There was no indication of when this would be, but the disease directly impacted his longevity. In my line of work, I find that, sadly, this is a time when most people finally give the matter of their will some thought. We all know there's nothing like fear to make you confront or face something that feels awkward, right?

Interestingly in this case, having absorbed his diagnosis (as well as possible), this gentleman felt a great need to make plans to protect his family members. Ideally, this is done in your will or with your 'estate plan'. Carefully thinking about the needs (especially financial) of those around you is an important step in this process. And this needs to be done way before you're lying on your death bed.

If you spend life accumulating wealth, you need to give it some direction before you die. Please don't leave this until it's too late (and remember: you don't know when it will be too late...because it will be *too late*.)

> ## *We know death is inevitable at some point, so don't shy away from planning for it now.*

Why you need a Will

First things first. If nothing else, get yourself a Will. According to the Australian Research Council, 60 per cent of Australians have a Will and many of these are inadequate.

It's important to know what will happen to your money when you die. It's really about paving a path for your family to manage when your time on this planet ends. (FYI: while I am a subject-matter expert in the area of estate planning, I am not a lawyer and I do not write Wills for my clients.)

Here's a really good example and reason why you need a well-documented Will.

Sam's legacy

Recently, I was talking to a gentleman named Tom. He is one of three siblings. His parents are in their late 70s and they live in regional New South Wales.

Twelve months ago, Tom lost his twin brother, Sam, to cancer after a two-year battle. Many discussions had been had among the family members relating to Sam's wishes when he died. Things such as who he wanted to inherit his property, and how he wanted to give money to his parents and surviving siblings (Tom and Matt). Yet, in mysterious circumstances (mysterious to the family), Sam's female carer became the full and only beneficiary of his estate (which, of course, sparked all kinds of speculation about whether this occurred while Sam was under the influence of pain medication).

The family were, understandably, shocked. The third brother, Matt, was the executor of Sam's estate. Promises had been made to both Tom and his parents by Sam that weren't documented, which they only discovered after Sam died. Being the executor, Matt followed what the will said — he had no choice.

Apart from dealing with the pain of their loss, this led to much confusion, upset and drama in the family. As a result of Sam's Will (perhaps inadequately reflecting what the family expected it to say), Tom said, 'I will never talk to Matt again'. This has caused such a significant rift in the family that it is unlikely to heal during the rest of their lifetime.

Unfortunately, this kind of situation is not that uncommon.

More than 50 per cent of wills are contested in Australia every year because family members thought they might be entitled to something in a will that they did not receive or because they were not considered in the drafting of the Will. Reg Grundy, Richie Benaud, Peter Brock, Bob Hawke and Neville Wran are just a few well-known Australians whose estates were contested by family who were not included in their last Will. Legal fees can rip sharkbite-size chunks from an estate through different sides wishing to get a better financial outcome for themselves.

The lesson in Sam's story is not about who was the right person to be the executor of the Will, nor whether Sam was in his right mind when he decided to give his wealth away to his carer.

> ## *The lesson is that you must have a will: a good, well-thought-out and well-documented will, down to the finest detail.*

Be upfront with others involved

Dying without a Will is very messy and you risk your hard-earned money going to the government if your family doesn't claim it. (And no-one wants that!)

Carefully planning your will isn't easy, especially if you don't know what everyone's needs are. Family members don't talk about this stuff among themselves. You don't hear people say:

- 'How much have you got in the bank?'
- 'Do you know how long that will last?'
- 'How much do you earn?' (okay, maybe some people ask this one)
- 'Do you have any investments and if yes, what are they?'

- 'Do you have one house or more?'

- 'How much are you worth?'

However, one of the key steps in planning your will is to know the answer to each of these questions, in detail.

You can develop a new relationship with your family when you have these conversations. Rather than just considering where all your hard cash goes when you die, contemplate this according to the needs of family or your community as well.

By sharing your answers to these questions openly and transparently with your family, you can actually foster a stronger and more positive relationship with money between you all.

For example, I worked with a couple who were self-funded retirees. They were in their 70s and had moderate wealth, mostly tied up in real estate (which is fairly typical of the boomer generation). There was nothing overly complex to consider in their estate. They had two adult children in their 40s with whom they had a good relationship, so it felt natural to appoint their kids as their executors.

This opened the door to discussing the needs of the whole family, including their children and grandchildren. It was clear that to fund retirement, they would need to sell some real estate, which their kids actually encouraged them to do (and in turn helped them do). The focus became on the grandchildren, who could be looked after down the track. This in turn influenced the estate plan and the will, and they created a testamentary trust for the grandchildren so that future education could be funded tax effectively.

In addition, for the first time, the family discussed their philanthropic interests and came together on something that would help a particular charity as a whole family rather than just a single generation. This opened up a new discussion not just about the parents' legacy, but everyone involved—their children, grandchildren and the wider community. (What a difference this story is from Sam's one, right?)

When you take the time to consider these questions, develop your answers and share this with everyone involved, it can open up another world for you in terms of making correct, fair and balanced decisions in the planning of your Will and your bequests.

Often the greatest grief comes from the lack of knowledge family have when someone dies, so include them in the planning process early.

How to hold a conversation about your Will

My secret party trick is to ask a really awkward question: 'Have you got a *current* Will?'

I emphasise the use of the word 'current' for effect as most often Wills are prepared decades apart and are well out of date by the time they become relevant.

Usually when I ask someone this, my family and friends roll their eyes behind my back, and I do get a few blank (scared) stares back.

But in my experience, it works a treat as an ice breaker because it's so unusual. (People might assume I'm an undertaker or work in a morgue, though others think I'm some sort of lawyer after a quick buck.)

Personally, I take this question really seriously and there's good reason. I get to experience the dark side of inheritance, the risk of poor or no planning and the spanner this throws in the mix. It needs thinking time and, by equal measure, if you are going to give someone money when you die (from your estate) what are they supposed to do with it when they get it? Can they spend it on a holiday or should they pay off a mortgage? Do you even care? (*Tip*: you should!)

First up, understand these key terms and their roles in estate planning.

Will	A legal document that clearly sets out your (the testator's) wishes for the distribution of your estate after you pass away. It's a revocable written document. It designates who will control and receive your assets and belongings after you die, as well as who will supervise the distribution and management of your estate.
	For a Will to be effective and withstand any challenges, it must meet certain legal requirements in the way it is written and witnessed.
Estate	All assets (things owned) and liabilities (things owed) by you. This would generally include all your assets, such as houses, shares, life insurance, cash and personal items, such as paintings and jewellery, and in certain circumstances, your superannuation.
Beneficiary	A beneficiary is a person who will receive the benefit of a gift under a Will. You may name as many or as few people as you wish. You may also name charities, universities or schools to receive a gift under your will.
	Bear in mind, there is plenty of evidence for ill-considered Wills. If you don't provide adequately for your dependents, they may bring a family provision application to try to claim part of your estate.
Executor	The executor is the person (or persons) who you appoint in your will to oversee the distribution of your assets after your death. This person is likely someone who has been in your personal finance village for a long time. I see this person as the most important decision that you can make.
	Do make sure you confirm that they accept the appointment.
	It's worthwhile considering the following:
	♦ Is the executor able to be independent in their actions?
	♦ Is the executor able to act impartially?
	♦ Is the executor familiar with your wishes and your family?
	♦ Is the executor completely trustworthy and able to maintain confidentiality?
	It is also sensible to ensure you have a back-up plan. Appointing one or more executors will assist with this and it is common that someone close to you is your first choice, followed by a professional, such as your lawyer or accountant.
Probate	The official recognition by the Supreme Court that a Will is legally valid.

Power of attorney	A legal document that allows you to appoint a person(s) to manage *financial and legal decisions* on your behalf.
	An enduring power of attorney continues even if you lose the ability to make decisions for yourself.
Enduring guardian	A person you appoint to make *health and lifestyle decisions* on your behalf if you become unable to, due to injury, illness or disability.
Testamentary trust	This is a trust created in your Will that operates in a similar way to a discretionary family trust. When considering the terms of your will, there are benefits of using one of these if you have young children or significant assets.
Advanced care directive	This is a legal document that deals with your future health care. You can give directions about your medical treatment for when the time comes when you cannot speak for yourself.

Next, get yourself well prepared for a consultation to prepare your will into an official document with a lawyer. Here are your nine conversation starters:

1. Do you have a trusted advisor, such as someone from your personal finance village or a close family member, you can discuss this with (this could be the family accountant or lawyer if it's not a family member)?

2. Can this person be your executor (that is, carry out the wishes contained in your will once you die)?

3. Do your family understand your wishes as they stand today? If not, take time to explain the implications of what you are doing (no-one likes surprises!).

4. Who will benefit from your wealth when you die? Make a list of the specific family and friends, charity or other.

5. Do the people benefiting have the skills to deal with a sizeable amount of money or wealth? If not, what skills can you equip them with today? Do they know how to invest money and if not, how can you help them today? (Your network is key.) Is there someone you trust in your network who might be able to provide some guidance to them? (See point 1 above and also

beware the spendthrift or anyone who might not look after your money like you have been doing — more on that in the next chapter.)

6. Have you given your family the heads-up on your will (see point 3 above)? Talk to them about Great Aunty Gladys' teapot — for example, 'Does anyone specifically want this when I die?' (I once had an executor try to work out what to do with deep-sea French fishing rods because they weren't specifically mentioned in the Will. I have also witnessed many a fight about a watch and who owns it. Try to get solutions for these kinds of things now.)

7. Have you made adequate provision for taxes? Can you use a testamentary trust to reduce the impact of tax on your children or grandchildren? Do you even know what a testamentary trust is? (Most accountants can tell you how these work.)

8. Are you in a blended family and are you adequately providing for all children: blood and stepchildren?

9. Are you clear on how the money should be spent by your charity of choice when you die? Can you request something specific rather than a general donation — for example, funding research into brain cancer or buying a piece of medical equipment for a hospital?

When you've sat down to have this conversation with your family members, don't shove your answers in a drawer for eternity. Book an appointment to see an estate planning lawyer so they can commence drafting your will. In any case, it would be rare that you could nail this in one go. Everyone needs time to process this.

Check your will whenever something in your life changes (when I say 'check', I mean call your lawyer to book an appointment). I'd recommend every three years or when life circumstances change: a new child or grandchild, a new house, a new mortgage...you get my drift. Remember, it's not just your circumstances that change, it's those of your family too.

Share this information with your family. Make it 'alive', a living breathing document that is constantly reassessed and updated.

And if, right now, you're still at the point of *Oh yeah, I'll come back to this later... it's not as important as X, Y, Z... I'm not dying yet... it's all too hard and complicated...*, remember that we started this chapter having this same conversation.

Please trust me and *push on*.

A considered Will is better than no Will at all.

Here's why...

How to rest in peace

Globally, there are many famous disputed Will cases where family members have battled over how much money they want from an estate. Michael Jackson had a short, simple Will; Jimi Hendrix died with no Will; Whitney Houston had one beneficiary, who in turn died without a Will; Philip Seymour Hoffman had a 10-year-old Will that considered one child, but when he died he had three children; and James Gandolfini's poor planning led to 80 per cent of his assets being subjected to taxes (*eek!*).

Please don't leave a headache for your family and your executors. Will your legacy be a headache? Let's hope not. It does take time to secure a well-considered legacy, one that enables your wealth to transition to others in a straightforward, practical manner, free from complexity and worry wherever possible.

If there are pain points or unresolved issues, do what you can today to resolve them and then document the solution.

Your death — sorry (not sorry) to be so direct — is a certainty that you need to plan for. No more excuses: don't let the complications of your life, or your money story, get in the way of making a will.

Planning, transparency and communication are critical.

Planning your will now means dodging a disaster later — for you and everyone involved.

Rest in peace, please!

Stop worrying now

1. Consider how your family (e.g. spouse, children) will survive without you. Write a list of the things that you pay for and are responsible for now — for example, mortgage, food, education, care, housework. This is key to your estate planning; it helps inform you of the financial support you need to have in place so their ongoing needs can be met, even after you die (e.g. you might need to consider life insurance if you haven't already done so).

2. Write down any special needs of your family members — for example, school-aged children, a family member with a disability or an elderly relative.

3. List your assets *and* if there is anything sentimental that you would like to see in the hands of a specific person.

4. Name the charity or community organisation that you would like to give money to.

5. Make an appointment with an estate planning lawyer.

part II
dealing with worry

Part II highlights many of the unexpected events that happen in life and how they can impact you financially.

We'll look at the best way to tackle common worries such as separation, divorce, financial infidelity, gambling and addiction. We'll consider how to identify these and how to recognise the warning signs to reduce their impact on you and the complex issue of money.

We know with money comes power so we must also tackle the increasing incidence of financial abuse. We'll identify how to recognise it, the red flags in a relationship and how to plan an exit from a financially abusive relationship.

It's an important part of the book, not only for you but for someone you know — you might have a sibling, or a friend who needs support with this.

Chapter 7
Attend to relationship dramas and divorce

You've tried hard, for what feels like an eternity. There have been countless hours of counselling, or 'couples therapy', plenty of tears and you've come to the end of the road. You feel helpless and you know it's over.

Yep, I'm talking about your marriage; your relationship; your partnership (whatever form it takes).

You have that sinking feeling deep in your gut. As each day, week and month has gone past, you have more questions. There's a fear building inside. What does this mean...for you, the kids, your career, family and friends? What about the lovely home you've built together? And, of course, the plans you had for a pool and a holiday to the coast next year. And then there's your joint bank balance...Your money worries run deep.

Understandably, this is a really unsettling time — and we'll get to the emotions behind this in a minute. First, whatever your situation, I have to prepare you for an initial shock.

Unfortunately, for a lot of people, this is where they realise that only one person has been in control of all the finances.

Women, in particular, seem to start strongly, holding the purse strings. But then, as the years go on, they lose sight of the big picture. They get a new house, change jobs and just get 'busy'. So, the finances tend to fall to the wayside, and the other person picks up the slack…eventually. This is where your typical expense creep (which we discussed in chapter 1) becomes an octopus with tentacles everywhere. You know it's become complex and you need to get your head around it. No more delegating.

Just stop and think for a minute: do you actually know where all your money is invested, how much is owing on your credit cards, how many monthly subscriptions you have or how much your partner earns? (Don't laugh, I'm serious about that last one.)

Take Monica, for example.

Monica: a shocking revelation

I recently spoke to a very senior female executive who was divorced many years ago. It was an amicable separation. She retained the family home and continued to raise the children there. She recalled her surprise, and downright shock, when her now ex-husband purchased a fancy apartment up the road to live in. When she asked him how he could afford this $2.5 million seafront property, he said, 'The bank loaned me the money based on my salary', to which she replied, 'How much do you earn?'

Monica said to me, 'We didn't really talk about how much money each of us earned or what our salaries were. We just made it work'.

If you're married, you might feel like this too. It all works 'fine', until suddenly, one day, it doesn't — which is exactly where you may be now.

We are smart people. We don't think this is going to happen to us, so we put these essentials off until it's too late.

Someone else confided in me recently that they are contemplating separation. When it came to the question about his spouse's income, he didn't know the specifics, though he had a rough idea. And he was aware that his wife had stock options in the company she worked at, but was unaware of their value.

Whatever your role, background or gender, it's imperative to know these basics. Current statistics reveal that 33 per cent of *all* Australian marriages are expected to end in divorce, and countless more relationships fall by the wayside.

So it is in your best interests to have a handle on the family income, expenses and balance sheet at all times. That's why part I of this book is so important.

> ### There are steps you can take right now that will save you a lot of heartache in the long run.

Equal unhappiness

It's super important to take ownership of whatever situation you're in. You might feel like this is 'happening to you'. I suggest that you accept the feeling and focus on money from this point on, no matter how 'amicable' things might be. You need to be informed and on the front foot. No passengers allowed from here.

Whatever circumstance you find yourself in — whether you're kicking off a new relationship, mid-divorce or just considering a break-up — I recommend you get a great, reliable accountant who can help you understand what you've got and a family lawyer to guide you through all the options and paths to protect yourself and your wealth. (Remember that chapter 4 helps to guide you on adding the right people to your finance village.)

A little note here: it's likely that you share advisors with your soon-to-be ex-partner, so technically they will have a conflict. You might need to add someone new to your personal finance village.

Here's something really important you have to remember *now*:

Do whatever it takes to avoid ending up in court. It's extremely costly on both cash and wellbeing for all involved. Just as your relationship took time to build, so does the process of 'uncoupling'. I'll say it again — *do whatever it takes to avoid court.*

I often say, if at first you don't succeed, *try again*. I'm not talking about the relationship (you've already tried that part), I'm talking about managing your process of separation as respectfully as you can. Do your best to be reasonable. Ask a trusted colleague — someone who can be objective — what they would consider to be fair in the context of your financial separation.

There are mediation services you are required to use prior to going to court. Try as hard as you can to use as much energy as you have to work with this process. Mediation will ultimately lead to a better outcome than anything the court process will do — and it's quicker.

At the time of writing, the wait time for the family court to hear your case is up to two years in Australia... That's a lot of recovery time being used up waiting, notwithstanding the pressure to prepare countless affidavits, trawl through all of your relationship and financial history... and that's if you don't have kids. If there are children involved, the complexity goes through the roof if you head to court.

There's a motto that follows separation and divorce that you should carry with you always: 'equal unhappiness'.

This means if you think there is give and take in a relationship, wait until you try to exit one or an exit is forced upon you. It's tricky to get a 'win-win' or anything that feels like a win-win when you are essentially halving whatever you have built together financially, from the glassware and cutlery to the bank balance. Equal unhappiness is what you're aiming for.

Go for much more and you're likely to end up in court, unless the other party (your soon-to-be ex) rolls over. In my 30+-year career, I'm yet to experience a rollover. Unfortunately, family often get involved and it becomes emotionally fraught. Family can also fuel your soon-to-be ex-partner. In-laws have been known to muscle in on marriage breakdown, especially where their grandchildren are involved. Fierce family loyalty may show its face and really turn the heat up on any process you are trying to manage. This comes with the territory, so get comfortable with it.

An important word of warning here: domestic abuse or violence is often triggered by separation. This is *not* okay in any circumstance. Let the police know — don't be a silent victim.

Starting from ~~scratch~~ experience

Someone wisely once said, 'Don't be afraid to start over again. This time, you're not starting from scratch. You're starting from experience'.

So if you're potentially facing a break-up, you need to take control of where you're at and that means deciding which of these three scenarios you're facing:

♦ *Scenario 1: contemplation.* You're unhappy and thinking through whether this relationship should end (this is all in your court and your partner may be in the dark).

♦ *Scenario 2: amicable.* You're about to commence separation (you've amicably agreed to a split and now need to work together before formally appointing lawyers).

♦ *Scenario 3: courtroom drama.* You have left the family court, final orders in tow (you went the whole nine yards, likely acrimoniously, and your only key step now is to rebuild).

Keep this in mind as you move on to the next steps.

P.S. If you are the person who's been shuffling around in the dark, and realised your partner has just put the lights on and pulled the pin, then get onto the following asap.

Taking charge

As we've seen, it's not uncommon for one person in the relationship to take charge of the money — so, starting now, that needs to be you!

There are five financial steps you need to go through to become the controller of your finances, regardless of your scenario or personal circumstances.

It's time to take charge now.

You might feel that you need to do this discreetly if you need time to think through how all of this might impact you. That's pretty normal. I often speak to people in relationships and they just need to get a start on understanding their money so they can appreciate and plan for where they might end up when the relationship is over.

Follow these five steps:

1. Work out what you've got

2. Value what you've got

3. Determine the split

4. Complete the transfer

5. Rebuild.

Let's look at each in turn.

1. WORK OUT WHAT YOU'VE GOT

Bottom line, you need to be informed. In my experience, it's rare for both people in a relationship to take responsibility for money matters. At this point, it doesn't matter who that is, but you need to become familiar with all things money.

Often the first task is to locate your assets. By this, I mean understand how each asset is owned—which bank it is with, how it is structured (for example, the number of shares)—and look for any critical documentation, such as:

- bank account numbers

- names on investments and types of investments

- names on the title deeds of any property

- names of financial institutions the accounts and investments are with

- names and numbers of *all* credit cards

- frequent flyer accounts and total points balances

- the constitution and shareholders of any businesses you own

- trust details and deeds

- insurance policies (e.g. for cars, house, furniture, life, income protection, TPD).

Once you've got this info, you can move on to the second step.

2. VALUE WHAT YOU'VE GOT

Now it's time to value all of your joint assets. Write down the dollar value against the items listed above and any new items mentioned here. We are building a joint balance sheet, which will be the basis for a financial separation.

So, put a dollar value next to each of the following items:

- every bank account

- every credit card debt

- an estimate of your home's value (you can search for this online)

- your current bank debt

- each item of significance: household furniture, jewellery, artwork, cars and expensive toys (e.g. jet ski or snowboard). What would someone pay for these items today in their current state?)

- every company and trust: Who has the shareholding? Did you pay for it in any form? If you paid, add this price to your joint balance sheet

- the last two to three years' profit if you're in business with your partner — write down the average for three years then multiply this by 3. In addition, look at the financial statements and *net* assets and make a note of this in your joint balance sheet.

Add it all up.

Once you have a total estimated dollar value, multiply that by 50 per cent. That's a good place from which to start preparing yourself. You may be in shock at this point. Most Aussies have so much wealth tied up in their family home that it becomes a real barrier to ending an unhappy relationship. I get it, but is this the price of your happiness?

3. DETERMINE THE SPLIT

What the split should be is anyone's guess right now. Working with 50 per cent is a good benchmark.

Is it amicable? If you're in scenario 2 (see 'Starting from ~~scratch~~ experience' above), you may be able to meet somewhere in the middle. A lot will depend on the type of dynamic between you at this stage in your relationship.

Beyond this point, you've got to look at the big picture. If your mind is made up and you feel the split should be 60/40 in your favour because you took time off work to raise the kids and stay at home, consider how much 10 per cent of, say, $3 million would be ($300 000). I can guarantee you, if you head to court over $300 000 because your partner doesn't agree with your suggested split, you'll spend that $300 000 in court and legal costs. *Think again.* Remember: *big picture.*

You might have a net balance sheet of $1 million or $15 million, but do your maths. I am yet to meet a couple post court who feel like winners.

A note on superannuation: women typically retire with 23.4 per cent less super than men, according to The Association of Superannuation

Funds of Australia (ASFA). Couple this with women's longer life expectancy and it's worthwhile taking the opportunity through your divorce to even up your super. It's the one time when you can transfer super without ugly tax considerations.

And remember: 'equal unhappiness'.

4. COMPLETE THE TRANSFER

Bite the bullet: sell what needs to be sold and move on. It's easy to be sentimental, but it also makes the recovery really difficult. Starting fresh will be good for your state of mind (in time).

If they have children, one parent often considers staying in the family home to reduce the devastating impact on the kids. I wouldn't recommend this path. The kids need you to comfort them, and being in the same house with only one parent isn't the same. You might also be hanging onto broken dreams. This is a hard time, even if it's your call to leave.

So when I say 'fresh start', I mean a new outlook for the kids as well. It's going to be different from here on. From the minute you wake up until the moment your head hits the pillow at night, it will be different. The routine of life — whether it's the cooking, the dishwasher stacking, school drop-off, grocery shopping, taking the bins out or mowing the lawn — will look and feel very different.

You want to create something that engages you and the kids no matter what age they are when you separate. You might create a new routine, again depending on their age. It might be going to the movies together to watch a new blockbuster of their choice, or picking up the Xbox controller to see what that's all about or getting ice-cream on Fridays after school. This is a creative time for creative thinking and creative living, too.

5. REBUILD

This ain't easy, but you can do it. For so many years, most decisions will have been made by two adults, together. Now it's just you. Be brave and own it.

Get back to the basics from part I. Get your new house or rental in order. Every expense you have needs to be reframed. This stage will generally just be temporary. Over time, your income may go up or your income-earning potential may improve and you might meet a new partner, but for now, work with what you've got.

Going it alone does have an upside... you can do whatever you want within your means!

You really need to *reset* from a budgeting perspective too. You might be paying maintenance of some kind, or you might be in receipt of it. Either way, it won't feel like you have enough money. This is your time to get back to basics, work out what really matters and be savvy with your cash.

For those in scenario 3, if you've come this far and you've seen the inside of a court room, it's likely that the final decision on your wealth, money and care of the children has been made for you by a judge. This can be harsh. Following steps 1 to 4 results in an outcome that will be court directed for you. Step 5 is up to you.

This is when IKEA becomes your friend. When you need to furnish a rental or if you've been able to keep the family home, but the possessions have been split, you need to fill the gaps: beds, linen, couches, dinnerware, TV. This is good for the kids too; they can engage in this with you and they might be excited about something new. I appreciate that I'm being materialistic, but it might soften the edges a little.

Get your new house in order, whatever form that might take. You might have even moved back to your parents' house. This is a good time to restock, reflect and renew.

You're not broken: you're starting new.

A final word...

That word is *you*.

You may be facing all sorts of demons processing this separation or divorce. You may be re-joining the workforce for the first time in many years. You may be taking on debt that you wonder if you can repay in your lifetime. There may be fear, anxiety and genuine feelings of sadness and loss...this is all normal. These feelings will pass with time.

However, aside from your accountant and lawyer (who will feel like your closest friends for a while), I also recommend it's smart, not shameful, to have a counsellor or psychologist to provide you with much-needed strength as you work through your uncoupling.

You have heavy emotions you need to process. Finance, at this stage, often feels detached, even cold, but there is a harsh and logical reality in looking after yourself. Trust me that you don't want to get to five years later, in a new and improved relationship, and kick yourself for the financial mistakes you made during your separation.

Keep rational and have the right relationships you can draw on for emotional support.

Stop worrying now

1. Check in with how you are feeling right now. Have you done all you can and is it time to move on from this relationship?

2. If it's happening to you and you're not ready for it, take the time to identify people to add to your personal finance village who can help you, such as a lawyer, and look for a counsellor to support you through this. Who else can you ask to help you?

3. Set aside time to understand all your finances. You might feel overwhelmed at the start, but you need to do this now. Take the lead from step 1 in this chapter and understand where you stand.

4. Then take a look at your baseline costs from the chapter 1 activity. Have a think about what expenses you need to continue paying once you've separated. Make a list of these.

Chapter 8
Watch for and address money cheating

Financial infidelity feels as bad as it sounds and is a leading cause of relationship breakdown and divorce because it's a fundamental breach of trust. As many as one in three couples have dealt with financial infidelity in their relationships.

In its most basic form, *financial infidelity is when you or your partner lies about money*. It's money cheating and it occurs when one partner lies about how much they earn or how much debt they have.

Many households have become dual breadwinners over the past couple of decades, meaning people earn independent incomes and possibly have separate bank accounts, which has blurred the spending lines. You or your partner's spending habits can be well hidden. In some cases, debt can escalate to the point where serious intervention is required. Your accounts get frozen because your bills haven't been paid—or worse, the bailiff (aka enforcement agent) turns up on your doorstep.

The act of financial infidelity can be so well masked, it may go unnoticed for a long period of time, which is why it's important to be aware of anything out of sorts before it becomes an issue for you or your household.

But remember, this isn't about pointing the finger of blame. It's about identifying it, understanding why it happened, addressing it and then working towards a solution, with your partner, so that it doesn't happen again.

Are you heading for a shock?

Picture this. You open the mail one day and make a very unromantic discovery. While you are across the family finances, unbeknown to you, your partner has been racking up credit card bills and a final notice has been posted to your home.

You had both committed to a tight household budget, the mortgage was taking a fair chunk of your income and it seemed your lifestyle costs had exploded in recent months.

You had agreed to postpone your plans for a holiday to Hawaii to try and get on top of the baseline of costs that had crept into your lives and to try to pay off your existing credit card debt (before the one you just received by post).

You had both committed to sticking to a budget to save an extra $500 per month.

It turns out your partner was piling on credit card debt to treat themselves. You felt guilty because you saw one of the purchases was a gift for you.

You pluck up the courage to raise this with your partner and leave the opened notice on the kitchen bench. When it comes time to discuss it, they wave it off, make fun of it and say, 'Oh yeah, I've had that for years, long before I met you. Just hadn't bothered to close it'. You ask another probing question: 'Do you use it?' Your partner says yes...and that's the end of it. Or is it?

This may be the first sign of financial infidelity in your relationship. It's a relatively common scenario and if this, or something like this, has happened or is happening to you, don't fret immediately; there is a bit to work through.

Take the time to have an open and honest conversation with your partner about money (this might be new for you both). You both might be carrying some excess money baggage that has led to this so check in first to ensure everything is okay.

Relationships are built on trust, and we tend to take things for granted so see this as an opportunity for your relationship rather than a threat.

Beware the warning stories and signs

When we enter relationships, we enter with our own level of financial independence and awareness. Over time, your level of financial independence can become blurred when it comes to spending. You begin to share financial information such as your salary, credit cards and other debts with your significant other. It gets trickier to maintain your level of financial independence as you merge lives and bank accounts without talking openly about your spending habits.

In addition to this, your own experience with your parents (or money baggage, as I refer to it) may have an impact here. Did your parents have everything in joint accounts? (You may have assumed this if money was never really discussed when you were growing up.) It worked as far as you were concerned so why wouldn't it work for you, right?

We know it can start with the little things. Your partner buying small indulgences online such as clothing, accessories and other indiscriminate feelgood spending without telling you. Those impulse buys can be harmless, but they can also cause trust issues, especially when they disrupt the household budget.

Down the track a little, you might even agree to let your partner deal with the money matters for both of you. (Massive red flag here!)

I can't emphasise enough how important it is that you retain a level of financial independence in terms of knowledge about your income, your expenses and your partner's when you're under one roof.

With your partner in charge of managing the household outgoings, it makes it relatively easy for them to keep their spending secret. For you, it may just be the credit card; for others it can be far worse. People's lives get turned upside down and back to front in cases of financial infidelity and when they regain their financial literacy it's too late: the damage is done and you're in a crisis.

Have you ever told a little white lie to your partner relating to a purchase? You're not on your own. If this is something you are doing often, or your partner is doing often, you need to get to the bottom of it. Those little indulgences (sins) start small: you remove price tags before your partner sees them or you simply suggest something is 'an old thing' that you've had stashed in the cupboard for a year rather than acknowledging it as a new purchase...

It sounds like a sitcom or a Hollywood movie. Actually, there have been movies showcasing these types of behaviours or habits. I recall seeing Isla Fisher in the movie *Confessions of a Shopaholic* attempting to deep freeze her credit cards to curb her out-of-control spending. I've also witnessed friends literally cut up credit cards because they can't stop using them, running up debts and wreaking havoc with their ability to save. It can be manageable when you set clear expectations about how they are used, but when you don't know your partner is spending on a card it can spiral.

The key to preventing financial infidelity is to have joint management of money matters in your household.

Seven money sins to recognise

Money lies take several forms, but most commonly they are:

- secretive purchases (buying stuff)
- secretive spending (like gambling)
- frivolous spending
- hiding debts
- dishonesty about income
- secret bank accounts
- secret investments.

Don't be the victim of your own complacency in a relationship. Taking responsibility for your financial health is good for your wellbeing. Delegating money matters comes with known risks — and some potentially unknown ones, such as those mentioned above.

Over time it can be difficult to regain financial literacy over things you have long forgotten. You need to know where your money goes (in and out the door) and you need to understand your investments — that is, everything you share or don't share with your partner.

Watch for these financial infidelity red flags:

- new credit card statements — that you know nothing about
- new bank accounts — that you know nothing about

- new items appearing in your house that you didn't buy or see on a statement somewhere

- frequent packages arriving at home addressed to your partner

- new passwords

- unwillingness to discuss money matters

- your partner's behaviour when you raise money doesn't pass the smell test (i.e. it doesn't seem authentic to you)

- your partner making money decisions without consulting you

- your partner being paranoid about you opening the mail.

What if you spot a money cheater in your household?

It can be upsetting at first to discover that your partner is a money cheater. You are likely to feel betrayed and angry. Planning to raise the issue will be really stressful, but there are three critical steps you can take:

1. *Ask, listen and support.* The first step is to ask your partner to come clean on their money lies. Be curious and listen. You might discover that your partner has avoided sharing their spending with you, they might be embarrassed, or they might feel judged or ashamed. This is not an excuse, but it's helpful to know and understand where they are at.

2. *Get help.* Your partner might need some help (from a professional) to address their spending. It's likely the spending has escalated over time for them. In planning a way forward together you might like to re-affirm your views about money and trust in a relationship as a starting point and then work towards jointly striving for complete transparency about money and spending going forward.

3. *Reconcile the steps forward.* We know financial infidelity is likely to reduce or destroy your trust in your partner. Reconciling

'cheating' and dishonesty may be difficult, and it would be worthwhile considering getting counselling to help you work through this with your partner. If you are both willing to work together, it will go a long way to healing the hurt and reducing the risk of future money sins.

What if your partner/parent/child is gambling?

Sometimes money cheating goes very bad.

Australia is known as a gambling nation. By way of example, the turnover of poker machines in New South Wales alone was greater than $54 billion in 2019–2020 and that was during the disruption of a pandemic! More than one-third was gambled in council areas with low-income households. One in five people experience problems with alcohol, drug use or gambling during their lifetime. Can you begin to imagine the pressure those families would be under managing their cost of living?

Around 80 per cent of young people also participate in gambling at least once. On average one teen in every high school class has an issue with gambling.

On a personal note, I have witnessed many gambling addicts go too far, reaching a point where the entire family's wealth was eliminated. I've also seen young adults bet every dollar they have to compete with mates on a Saturday at the races.

Tom and Liz: when gambling becomes an addiction

Tom, a tradie in his mid 30s, had long enjoyed gambling for entertainment: playing Keno at the club, betting on horses and football (same game multi) and playing the poker machines.

(continued)

Tom and his wife Liz had an understanding that it was okay for Tom to gamble to an agreed limit. It's probably fair to say Liz never directly checked up on this...until it all came crashing down.

Tom's gambling had gotten out of hand. He had taken cash advances on all his credit cards (paying interest in the high 20 per cents), borrowed cash from one local to pay back another local and in turn, borrowed from another local (who may have been in a gang). Things continued to escalate to the point where Tom couldn't see a way out. Credit cards were maxed out and there was nothing left of his pay. It was becoming evident that he couldn't manage it. At this point Tom made a failed attempt at committing suicide and was fortuitously located by local police, and it all came to a head. The police brought Tom home. He was evidently a wreck. It was then that Liz discovered he had been covering up his gambling addiction for years.

Most people don't recognise that they have a gambling problem until it's too late. In my experience, most people who gamble deny there is any addiction. In fact, people who have a problem with gambling often lie about their betting habits or try to hide them from others. If you're in a relationship with a gambler, it's likely the spending (gambling) is kept a secret.

Statistically, around one in 20 Australians have an addiction (tobacco, alcohol or other drugs). From a financial perspective, it can take a massive toll on you and your family. In 2022, Australians spent $10.3 billion a year on illicit drugs (according to the Australian Criminal Intelligence Commission). That's an awful lot of cash missing from families' household budgets. Add to this that Australians gamble approximately $25 billion a year and it's clear that the financial ramifications are significant. What's more, it's reported that problem gamblers in low-income households spend 10 to 27 per cent of their household income on gambling.

Addicts are experts at covering up their habit, whatever it might be. Parents have been known to commit financial infidelity to support their adult children with addictions and to keep this financial support secret from their spouses. Children are known to blackmail their parents emotionally or become abusive if their parents don't give them the money they need. The longer this goes, the deeper the rabbit hole. All I can say is, if this is you and if you have bailed them out, paid a gambling debt and/or enabled an addiction, you both need support. You are not responsible, and you can't cure them. Your adult child must take accountability for their own life, and getting help is the best thing you can do.

If you're worried that you, a relative or a friend might have a gambling addiction, here are some common signs:

◆ You think or talk about gambling all the time.

◆ You spend more money or time on gambling than you intend to.

◆ You gamble when you feel sad, anxious or distressed.

◆ You spend more and more money to get the same 'kick' or rush.

◆ You bet more and more money to try and make up for past losses.

◆ You've repeatedly tried to stop or reduce your gambling without success.

◆ You become irritable or restless when you try to cut back on your gambling.

◆ Gambling is having a negative effect on your relationships, work or study.

◆ You rely on other people for money because of your gambling losses.

◆ You feel depressed or are having suicidal thoughts.

I'm not providing medical advice here, but I do suggest that if you are experiencing any of the symptoms described above, or someone close to you is, please do seek support. There is an abundance of organisations offering support for gamblers and their families (refer to the section 'Where to go for help' at the back of this book).

There is also some immediate action you must take to prevent any financial fallout.

If you are, or suspect that your partner is, suffering from an addiction, it's important to put as many safeguards in place as possible to reduce the likelihood that you become financially impacted by the addiction. You must act quickly at the first sign that this could be an issue. Your actions can protect your finances more quickly than the time it will take for someone to address their addiction. Many of our financial institutions are better geared now to assist too.

Do everything you can to ringfence your finances from the person who is suffering from the addiction:

- If you have any joint accounts, close them.
- If you are jointly liable on credit cards, exit them.
- If they ask for money, don't give it to them.

Again, seek qualified support sooner, rather than later.

How to avoid financial infidelity happening to you

Of course, the best way of addressing any kind of money cheating is to avoid it from the get-go. There are some really simple things you can do in your relationship to maintain honesty and trust on a regular basis when it comes to financial matters:

- Set regular times to catch up with your partner to discuss spending.

- Make talking about money more normal in your house (for example, talk about your bank balance, who is paying a bill or what bills you've just paid, what you'd like to buy and how you plan to buy it, what your plans are for your savings, how your super fund is performing and so on).

- Check in on your money goals together. Look over them and make sure you are on the same page. (Working through chapters 1 and 2 as a couple is a good start.)

- Add someone to your personal finance village to help with this, such as an accountant or financial advisor who can independently sit down with you and your partner to support open money discussions (see chapter 4).

- Enable 'safe' confessions (have a no-judgement rule for raising money sins). Allow yourselves the opportunity to come clean on spending and work out how best to address this going forward.

- Don't delegate your household money matters to your partner entirely.

- Up your game, and continue to read books like this one! Build your financial literacy.

- Don't let any difference in incomes make you feel uncomfortable (while this is common, creating financial goals together so that you are both aligned, as well as recognising the other contributions you make to the relationship, solves this).

- Always feel empowered to ask money questions. There is no such thing as a stupid question. The more you make money conversations the norm in your home, the better. If you're in doubt, do some research and then ask questions!

- Agree to make equal contributions to separate accounts so that you can indulge a little without recrimination.

Stop worrying now

1. Take a moment to consider your money relationship with your partner. Is talking about money the norm in your relationship?

2. What steps can you take to bring practical money discussions to your home? For example, reviewing monthly credit card bills together, discussing saving for something together. How might you go about it in terms of spending less (see page 15)?

3. Do you have a money sin that you would like to confess to your partner?

4. What are three things you can do tomorrow to tighten up or reduce the risk of money cheating happening to you?

Chapter 9
Know when it's money abuse

With money comes power. And sadly, that means nearly all cases of domestic abuse involve some kind of financial abuse. This is different from money cheating, which we covered in the previous chapter.

It's no longer financial infidelity when one partner controls the money and/or doesn't allow you to spend it without their approval — it's financial abuse. It's likely you will be tricked or trapped from accessing money completely in a financially abusive relationship.

Let's look at a hypothetical situation.

Jane: surviving financial abuse

Jane is a professional woman and entrepreneur. Two years ago, she relocated interstate for her husband's job. She had to quit her job to make the move and dropped her side hustle to manage all the complications of the move. Once they had relocated, she found it difficult to find a new job even though she was constantly sending her CV out to businesses. She was quite stressed for

(continued)

several reasons, one being that they had been undergoing IVF, which was an expensive and time-consuming process.

While she was at home, her husband encouraged her to do just that — stay at home — and started giving her a budget for the groceries. She made quite an effort to stay within the budget and also looked for regular specials when planning the weekly meals.

They were very relieved to find out the last IVF treatment was successful and began making plans for the long-awaited arrival of their first child.

The expectation of managing everything to the same budget after the baby was born was becoming increasingly difficult and Jane's partner began surveilling her on grocery shopping trips. He also discouraged Jane from spending money without him being around, although he didn't say it quite like that. Then he began asking for receipts for any shopping when he couldn't be there to supervise her. Jane didn't have any visibility over their bank accounts or his spending.

Jane confides in you and tells you about her worries. She has found that the financial abuse has become a lot worse since the baby arrived. The decision to become a stay-at-home mum was an easy one at the time because her husband earned much more than she did, but she regrets this decision now. It has made her feel isolated. She has become completely reliant on her partner for basic financial needs. He had slowly cut her off from their joint bank accounts, and convinced her that he should take control of their finances. She had naively handed the finances over because she trusted him. But now she feels trapped and is scared to leave.

Sadly, this story demonstrates how financial abuse can lurk within what appears to be a seemingly normal relationship to a bystander. What makes this so difficult, is that there is no freedom — only power and extreme vulnerability.

Beware of gaslighting

Your partner controlling money, or not allowing you to spend it without their approval, is financial abuse. It can be defined more broadly as follows:

- It is perpetrated precisely to trap someone.

- It is a tactic used by one person in a relationship to gain power and control by limiting access to money, assets and family finances.

- It comes in many forms, often discreetly, unable to be seen and difficult to pinpoint.

- It involves coercing and gaining control over a partner during episodes of domestic violence or relationship breakdown.

- It is a form of domestic abuse and is commonly perpetrated with domestic violence.

Gaslighting is a tactic associated with financial abuse. It's used to describe a form of psychological manipulation where the abuser attempts to create self-doubt or confusion in their partner to gain control over them. I'm sure you can sense from Jane's story that her confidence was waning, from starting as an independent, professional woman to someone essentially kept at home, with a baby, without access to money. Her partner has made efforts to isolate her from her network.

A classic case of gaslighting where money is concerned is when a partner steals money from you and then suggests that you lost it yourself (planting those seeds of doubt and, over time, reducing your confidence).

It's only in the past few years that we are gaining a better understanding of the gravity of financial abuse and the impact it is having on the community. It has only recently made its way into our media and it's great to see it talked about more because, as you will discover, it's more prevalent than you realise.

Sobering statistics

Aside from the devastating personal impact, the costs of financial abuse in Australia were recently estimated by Deloitte Access Economics to be $5.7 billion as a direct impact on victims and in addition to this, there is another $5.2 billion in costs to the economy from the reductions in victims' productivity and mental health. That's a staggering total of $10.9 billion.

Here's a summary of the $5.7 billion costs to victims:

$3.2 billion Withholding or controlling victims' income or finances

+ $1.2 billion Refusal to contribute to shared household bills

+ $0.6 billion Refusal to contribute to shared expenses for children

+ $0.6 billion Liability for joint debt

= **$5.7 billion** TOTAL

For the year 2020 alone, it was also estimated that more than 620 000 individuals were subjected to financial abuse.

> *This is something to worry about, and it is something that we all need to be aware of and address.*

Recognise the signs of financial abuse

Financial abuse is often hidden or hard to recognise.

Would you know how to spot these red flags?

- Limiting your access to cash, bank accounts or benefits
- Instituting an 'allowance' you're not okay with

- Making it difficult for you to get or keep a job, study or earn money (or sabotaging your job search)

- Not letting you work outside the home

- Interfering with your performance at work by showing up during work hours

- Persuading you to take out debt in your name that you're not going to benefit from

- Opening credit card accounts under your name

- Refusing to pay child support or help with childcare

- Completely controlling how the household income is spent and giving you an unreasonable amount to pay household bills and expenses

- Monitoring what you spend or asking to see all the receipts

- Forcing you to withdraw money from your superannuation

- Taking money from your wallet without asking.

One appalling ruse is where a financially abusive person opens an account (such as a credit card) under their partner's name and then gives their partner the credit card, expecting them to use it to pay for everything. Later, when the relationship breaks down, the card gets cancelled because no-one is paying the bills. The unsuspecting partner is landed with the credit card debt, which is in their name, and is left to pay the debt.

It's likely this person feels isolated and their confidence has been knocked out of them. The abuse would have developed over time, and they might be terrified and angry that their partner had the power to ruin their livelihood. The disruption to their children's lives would be a grave concern, and the issue becomes about self-preservation and possibly survival.

If this should happen to you, it's critical that you seek advice and tell your friends what is happening to you. Can you create some space from what is happening to you (perhaps visit a relative)? Talk to the police. They will be able to give you advice.

Yes, this will be difficult and may sound extreme, but leaving *right now* might be the safest and most practical thing to do.

Financial abuse is a crime in Australia and is recognised in all states and territories as a form of domestic abuse or violence (except for New South Wales, which at the time of writing is in the process of enacting new laws to criminalise it).

> ### *It's of the utmost importance that you protect your safety (and your children's) and finances (however limited they might be).*

Plan an exit

Cast your mind back to Jane's story, recognising that the red flags listed above would have enabled Jane to take some practical steps that would have set her up for an exit sooner.

Here is some suggested action to take if you're preparing to exit a financial abuse situation:

- Talk to someone you can trust. Tell them what's going on. They are likely to be able to assist with the points that follow and give you the support you need in taking steps to leave.

- Make copies of important documents such as your passport, bank statements, rates notices, deed of home ownership and any trust deeds. Print emails or take screen shots of messages from your partner relating to financial abuse. If you have a journal where you have recorded your experience, copy that too and move all of this evidence to somewhere out of the home (with someone you trust or a lawyer).

- Establish a bank account in your own name if you can. You will need some of the documents listed above to pass the identification test.

- Build your personal finance village: identify new advisors such as a lawyer (make sure they are independent of your relationship to ensure confidentiality).

- Re-connect with your professional network: people you worked with, colleagues, associates and people who know you professionally or in a work context. In time they may be the best source of potential jobs for you (if you're not working) to help with getting back on track. They may also have known you before the financial abuse, which is good for your confidence.

- Speak to a counsellor. Locating a counsellor who has experience with financial abuse will be an important resource for you to lean on both before, during and after the exit.

- Find a support group. Many survivors of financial abuse can give you support and encouragement and will have a network that you could tap into for other help.

- Consider building a side hustle or doing a bit of cash work while your partner is at work to put aside or in the bank account you have set up. You might not feel ready for this, but consider it an option. Doing something small and local (check out Airtasker for jobs people need help with — they can be simple one-offs) might help you build up a cash reserve that you otherwise wouldn't have.

While this list is not exhaustive, it's a place to start. Above all else, be careful. Take as many precautions as possible to protect yourself and call the police if you fear you're in danger.

It is difficult to leave a financially abusive relationship. Experts say financial abuse can be just as damaging as physical violence, but victims often don't receive the same support or sympathy.

If you think you are experiencing financial abuse, or a friend has come to you and you recognise the red flags, there are now many organisations (like those listed in the section 'Where to go for help' at the back of the book) that can support and help you with this.

> *Financial abuse violates trust, confidence, security and safety, and destroys relationships.*
>
> *Abuse is abuse ... no matter what kind it is.*

A word on elder abuse

Elder abuse — that of the over 65s — is financial abuse when there is illegal or improper use of the financial resources of an older person. Family members (the main perpetrators) may become inheritance impatient and commit elder abuse. For example, property being transferred from a parent to a child on a promise that they can live in the house and be cared for; bank accounts being fleeced of thousands of dollars by trusted persons; or parents being moved into aged care on the understanding that family will continue to care for them financially. Other examples include moving the older person out of home without their consent, or coercing them into signing documents including loans, powers of attorney or wills.

You might be worried about someone you know being the victim of this insidious form of financial abuse — and with good reason. It's estimated that one in 10 Australians will be affected by elder abuse every year.

If you are aware of this happening, *please don't ignore it*. Make a record of what you know, talk to the police and suggest to the older person that they seek advice from someone independent (better still, take them to see a mediator or a lawyer who specialises in this). It can be a grey area, especially if the person has lost their capacity. See 'Where to go for help' at the back of the book for more help.

Stop worrying now

1. Consider the ways your awareness about financial abuse has been raised. Is there a friend or family member you can share this with as a first step?

2. Have a think about people in your life who may be suffering in silence. Can you reach out to see if they are okay?

3. Prepare for the unexpected. Take some time to collect your most important documents, make copies and store them in the cloud — this is an important step regardless of where you're at!

part III
planning for the future

Part III is about the fun stuff. But you're not ready for this until you've worked through the beginning of the book—that's important. Why? Because we want to make sure we don't create a new set of worries!

So once you're ready, let's consider what your future might hold. A sabbatical, a side hustle or a new business, or a tree- or sea-change to somewhere new?

We'll document the financial impact so that it achieves the goal you've set for yourself and your family.

And then we'll look at two other important issues: gifting to others and growing financial literacy with our kids! Let's look at how to continue a positive money cycle for generations to come.

Chapter 10
Schedule a sabbatical or break

I worked pretty much non-stop for 30 years across two of the largest professional service firms in the world, before I even considered taking a break. And you know what, I wish I had asked for a sabbatical sooner. (Talk to any of your friends and they'll very likely say the same thing.)

At the time, I was a partner in the business, and it wasn't 'the norm' to offer extended leave, whether for three months, six months or longer.

These days it's a different story. While every company is different, and there is no legal requirement to offer sabbaticals, organisations that do offer sabbaticals recognise it is part of what makes working for them attractive.

Sabbaticals support the longevity of careers because you return with a fresh perspective and passion that may have been exhausted by the demands of your career along the way.

While they are not the panacea for all of the stress our work + life can cause, sabbaticals go a long way towards a 'refresh'.

But back then, even entertaining the idea, let alone asking for it outright, seemed outrageous! *I mean, would they really give me three months off just like that? Who would take care of my tasks, or would they just mount up ready for my return?*

My husband had asked me some thought-provoking questions like, 'If money was no issue and you didn't have to worry about kids, what would you do next?', to which I answered, 'Spend six months in Europe!'

Gradually from that day on we started to verbalise the desire (only between ourselves initially) to have a sabbatical and planned the where, what and how. This was really quite hard! I was enjoying my career and I was on a great trajectory, so I didn't feel confident about taking time off to galivant around Italy and Spain. I was concerned about the impact on my career. Let alone the money.

There was a really complex set of worries swirling around in my head (as I've no doubt you would also feel). Questions like:

- How long can I afford to be away?
- How will I pay my rent or mortgage and bills at home?
- How much would I need to save to make it happen?
- What will happen to my business?
- Will my job really be waiting for me when I return?
- Am I going to have to sacrifice some luxuries to make it work?
- Is all the work going to pile up and wait for me while I'm gone?
- How do I really turn off the stress?

All these worries crossed my mind — over and over again! And when D-day came to ask for leave from work, I was so nervous about asking to take this break. It felt like torture. And so, as I was speaking, I found myself culling back the leave time to something like 11 weeks and I even offered to keep in touch and look after some of the higher needs clients *for no pay!*

Above all else, notwithstanding the wonderful memories we have of the places we visited, the food, the Mediterranean hospitality and the blue coastline, what I experienced upon my return (and the moral to my story) is that from a career or work perspective, life goes on with or without you. When people know you are returning, they get excited about re-engaging you. Picking things up with that renewed energy and a different perspective is good for you and everyone around you.

I can tell you from personal experience that most of your deep-seated worries from the early days of contemplating your sabbatical will melt away. With the right planning, you can make it work. Within three months of my return, I could say there were no residual money concerns. We made it work.

It won't be 'back to normal' straight away, but within a few short months (if planned well) you will manage to pay off the remaining costs associated with your time away, as well as the money spent while overseas, and get back into paying the mortgage/rent and other ordinary costs of living.

Now, in hindsight, I would have pushed for at least four months off. The actual pay-off from the time off made the money worries seem insignificant.

If you wait until you 'need' the break, it's unlikely you will make it work.

Planning is the key to alleviating any worries.

Don't leave it till it's too late

No-one wants to be or feel locked down in a job forever. Let's hope you don't have to adopt the 'quiet quitting' strategy in response to your demanding job to avoid burnout. Things have changed remarkably in the past 30 years, before which time taking a long break wasn't really a 'thing'. We have all seen the impact of hybrid working these past few years and more employers are adopting flexible work plans. If you're lucky enough to work with a business that is opening their mind to sabbaticals, then don't be afraid to ask.

> ### It's in your best interests to find out what your organisation will do, is willing to do or better yet does when it comes to any kind of leave outside annual leave or long service leave.

I'd say most people worry mainly about losing money (e.g. losing work-related or business income) when planning a sabbatical, but in addition to that are fears (and genuine anxiety) about losing career momentum or progression, job security, the next promotion or a pay rise. For some it might be losing your job, losing your ability to pay your mortgage or the possibility of going into debt. These are reasonable fears, but each can be addressed with good, solid planning.

It is possible to plan your sabbatical at any stage of your career, but it can also help to time it with a professional or personal goal so that it feels like you earned it. For me, it was when my eldest son had finished school. It may not be the ideal time when you've started a new job, for example, or just bought a new house with a huge mortgage. You need to be financially savvy to take this kind of a break. Make it count by getting your budget organised. Work out where you stand today financially, and how you will save for the lead-up. Always consider other ways you might be able to earn more money (thinking outside the box) and what kind of financial buffer you can create for your return.

Here's one example of a high-profile Australian who documented her sabbatical journey live on radio.

Kate: planning a sabbatical

Kate Langbroek (comedian and radio/TV presenter) took a sabbatical at a career peak on a top-rating radio show. Kate lovingly documented it in her book *Ciao Bella! Six Take Italy* and has done countless podcasts since returning sharing the ups, downs and virtues of a sabbatical. Kate decided to take her family (including four school-aged children) on a one-year sabbatical to Italy.

Kate and her partner wanted a reset from their all-too-busy life, and their eldest son had had a brutal three-and-a-half-year battle with leukaemia (he has been given the all clear). It was time to nourish family relationships and head away. Kate was determined to ensure the kids' education continued and part of deciding *where* to base themselves in Italy was about locating an international school close to their accommodation — one that participated in local sports. Factoring in the official start of the Italian school year was just one of the many logistical considerations. Kate set aside a good 18 months to plan their sabbatical.

Now before you scoff and say, 'Well she can *afford* to take that kind of break', hear me out. You don't *have* to move to the other side of the world and uproot your whole family in the process of taking a sabbatical (unless it suits you and your circumstances). There are many wonderful stories of Aussie families buying a caravan, packing up and heading off on the road around Australia cost effectively.

Kate also continued working and doing her live radio show for the first six months of the sabbatical and by her own admission this was exhausting. She felt 'ripped off' — and you might have too.

There's a lesson in here regarding planning and trade-offs. Do you work during your sabbatical? Are there boundaries to set?

Top 10 tips to start planning a break

For a successful sabbatical (aside from it being great for your mindset) here are 10 things to consider and steps you can take to help ease your money worries in the lead-up, and to make the return as comfortable as possible.

1. Research the business or organisation you are in

Find out if there is a history of offering sabbaticals. Are they mentioned in your contract? If you are an employee, you may have long service leave. What are you owed (if anything)? What are the conditions around your contract of employment, and can you locate someone who has had experience planning one of these in your organisation? For example, I located a partner in the business who had taken a sabbatical and asked as many pre-planning questions as I could. In terms of her experience with the firm, this gave me a level of comfort.

2. Give your company as much notice as possible

You'll need approval, and the earlier you can help organise options (such as finding a replacement), the better. If it's up to you to cover yourself, work out a project timeline with the business that will see projects wrapping up or being transitioned to others in your planned absence.

3. State your case

Understand your main reasons for taking a break, like 'Why now?' It's good to share more detail about the reasons for your sabbatical, such as a life or family event that's important to you. You will find people will be more supportive when they recognise the purpose behind your request.

4. Socialise with stakeholders

This is a big one and I can tell you that it gets easier the more times you say it. I certainly felt very awkward talking about it at first, but it was necessary. It's a good opportunity to sit down with people you work with and seek their input into how you might best manage your workload in the lead-up to your break. You will find they are likely to be the first people you will connect with when you return so you can plan how you will go about this as well.

5. Block out your diary

This is therapy...blocking your diary with a big 'out of office' feels great. If calendars are shared in your organisation, people who work with you will see this if they are trying to book something down the track. Use this as a planning tool as well. Set up a countdown and set some goals for things that need to be wrapped up before your last week or two in the office. Set up reminders for important things to do prior to your leave.

6. Prepare a mini budget for your time away

Think about accommodation and transport costs (see below for some suggestions). If you have any savings (at the time of the decision), what percentage might you commit *now* to the travel budget vs, say, lifestyle costs?

7. Consider the trade-offs

Be prepared to consider there might be some sacrifices to make this work or reduce a money headache that will grow as your sabbatical gets closer! I recall having to hand over a program I was really passionate about as the main deliverable occurred during my sabbatical. The business needed someone to take full ownership of it and it would not have been fair to hang onto this until I left only to take it back when I returned. Hanging onto this, during my sabbatical, may have led to greater income for me down the track but the sacrifice on my sabbatical time would have meant it was not the break I was planning. A different kind of trade-off would be making the decision that you won't go 'shopping' for the six months leading up to the break; or no Uber Eats, maybe no new tech or no more shoes. You can have fun with this and maybe there is a reward for you once you reach your destination.

8. Save now

Where will your savings be focused before you take leave (e.g. for the travel list)? Can you pre-pay any costs for your time away (this will also reduce admin while you're away). Commit a percentage of your income now to the travel budget.

9. Consider all the 'open your front door' costs at home

What won't be needed while you are away? Do you need your home to sit vacant while you are away? Is there an opportunity to make money from your home or at least get some help with the bills while you are gone? Have a think about all the costs we identified in chapter 1 with your baseline summary. Challenge each of these, and don't be afraid to cut loose on some of your expenses.

10. Balance education (within reason)

Can the kids miss some school? Do they need to join you on the whole trip? Find out whether their current school will allow no school fees to be paid while your children take a semester away. Also identify the costs of an international school (or similar) option, should this be a longer sabbatical with kids.

Recognise that you do need to give yourself some runway in the planning phase. I'd suggest 18 to 24 months is a good timeline to get planning, depending on how long you're going to be away.

Stop, start, continue

One of the hardest things to do when planning is unpacking and understanding the costs and expenses you might incur while you're on sabbatical. This is what keeps people up at night.

A practical exercise you can do to start exercising your money-planning muscle is a financial *Stop, Start, Continue* process in the lead-up to your break and beyond.

Here's how it works:

Stop: What financial outlays can you stop?

Start: What costs might you start incurring?

Continue: What finances will remain the same?

Here are some suggestions to get you started on trimming costs and planning for your sabbatical. What can you add or remove from these lists?

	Money savings	Your costs ($)
Stop	Subscriptions	
	Gym memberships	
	Newspapers and magazines if you get the paper delivered	
	Streaming services — most won't work overseas (unless you use a VPN, which can be tricky) so you will need a local subscription	

(continued)

	Money savings	Your costs ($)
	If you have a leased car, can you sell it?	
	If you're renting, agree to a termination-of-lease date	
	Total costs saved	

	New costs incurred and continued costs	Your costs or estimates ($)
Start	Storage costs if you are packing up your house	
	Can you Airbnb your home or have someone house sit to help pay the mortgage/rent?	
	When preparing your travel budget, include:	
	◆ Transport (plane/train/car/boat…)	
	◆ Accommodation	
	◆ Daily spending allowance (including food)	
	◆ Travel insurance	
	◆ Entertainment (e.g. tickets you might need for access to museums or for activities)	
	◆ Foreign currency exchange rates and understand the impact on your costs (you could exchange some currency in the new country but these days the costs of doing this may outweigh the benefits)	
	◆ Mobile service costs from your carrier, providers and chargers at your destination	

	New costs incurred and continued costs	Your costs or estimates ($)
Continue (look over your baseline from chapter 1)	Insurance	
	Essentials — but test every cost that you have and decide if it's needed while you are away (time consuming but worthwhile)	
	Total new and continued costs	

Consider the benefits to your whole family: the non-financial upside of this experience will be priceless!

A note for business owners

When you own your own business, the very idea of taking time out may seem out of reach. However, I have seen many successful business owners take a sabbatical and return to build a more profitable and enhanced business (in some cases, an entirely new business) with a stronger mindset and greater passion than they have ever had before.

This is a time when your personal finance village should be activated. A great way to start is by asking who in your network has done this before. Who can act as a guide and hold your hand to make this a reality?

Here are key questions you will need to consider and ask yourself first:

♦ How can my business model or structure change to assist me while I'm away? (If you've had a holiday before you may know what things can be done in your absence.)

♦ Do I need to hire someone who will fill my shoes? At what cost?

♦ Will the new person be able to generate new revenue or a different revenue stream for the business?

- Do I need an administration person to sift through my emails while I'm away and ensure that a bank of contacts is being built up for my return? Could they politely communicate with clients or respond to any queries advising that I am taking a well-earned break and will reconnect on a future date? This is so much more personal than a detailed 'out of office' message (which is an option as well).

- Can I save and plan to shut the business while I'm away (ever heard of hibernation)?

- Can I close my office, which is currently rented? (Plan your sabbatical around a lease ending to minimise any further disruption.)

- Is there a competitor I have a healthy relationship with that could potentially caretake for me?

After this, in terms of thinking through the money implications, you should:

- *review costs and revenue.* Sit down with your accountant (or your business partner, or a trusted advisor, or all three independently) to review all business costs and revenue sources, estimate what will *stop* or *continue* and mock up a 'sabbatical profit and loss'.

- *unpack each revenue source.* Can you identify new sources of revenue that might work while you are away? Brainstorm how to reduce *all* costs and what costs are a must so that when you return you have a baseline to build from. Note: your revenue may taper off as you get closer to heading away, so factor this in as well.

- *allocate savings from your profit.* Ensure a share of your profits every month are being set aside to save for your sabbatical.

- *eliminate non-essentials.* Identify costs from your business so you are running leaner wherever possible. Think about your bottom line over the previous 24 months. How can you increase your profitability?

- *make sacrifices.* What are the sacrifices (or trade-offs) you can make now for this bigger experience? Leasing cars? Renting office space? IT support? Air travel vs online meetings?

- *be a time warrior.* Challenge your time use. Are the activities you are undertaking focused on the highest and best (most profitable) use of your time?

- *review your tax obligations.* Make sure your tax obligations are up to date. No-one likes surprises and you don't want to be on a sabbatical and be told by your accountant that you have a big tax bill to pay. Make sure all compliance is up to date, as painful as this may seem.

Remember, you have backed yourself in your own business. I have no doubt you've made plenty of sacrifices along the way. Planning your sabbatical now will bring you more energy and enthusiasm for what's to come.

You deserve this.

Leave without pay (LWOP), with a twist

Of course, you don't have to be going on a holiday to take a break from work.

Jim: returning to his roots

A friend of mine, Jim, had been working in a fairly staid work environment for a long time. The choice to stay in this type of office was more about job security than job satisfaction, and a reliable, regular income to support his family. It ticked a lot of boxes...except one! His passions lay elsewhere. He wanted to

(continued)

work in the great outdoors, on the land. In truth, this was about returning to his roots. His family had owned a cattle property when he was growing up. He felt that he needed to explore this further, and an opportunity had arisen when a job came up on a farm owned by his family.

Jim was in a position where he had accrued long service leave and also worked for a company that offered leave without pay options (for up to six months). So instead of planning a holiday or a road trip around Australia (which more and more people seem to be doing), Jim took an extended break — or 'sabbatical' — from his existing job and used that time to pursue his career change. Much like you would a *gap* year!

The greatest benefit of this type of scenario is taking the time off from your main employment role to consider the alternative without losing income, as was the case for Jim. However, this may not be available to everyone.

Take care to check that your employer allows this. Many employment contracts will not allow you to seek paid employment elsewhere on their time. However, there may be a loophole. For example, if you are seeking a break to help family out in some way (or in their business) in a time of need, your employer may permit you to earn an income. Like in Jim's case, where it was approved because he was helping family out.

I've seen others do this successfully too. For example, seeking LWOP to help in a carer role for a family member or friend, or to develop your skills further with, say, an MBA (and maybe you need to earn some money while you're doing this — like working as a barista part-time).

You may choose to:

- renovate your house
- spend some time at home with family
- kick off a new degree

- do a photography course

- learn a new language

- put the finishing touches on your own new business

- develop your side hustle

- care for a relative who is ill.

Think job security vs job satisfaction.

Don't assume just because your employer doesn't offer benefits such as LWOP that they won't consider it based on your set of circumstances. If you believe in it, make your case.

Throughout my career I have been in a position to approve LWOP for employees of the business. For me it always felt like having time away was a brilliant development opportunity for the individual. Most of them travelled. It didn't cost the business while they were away and if they returned, we all benefited. Not all of them did return, but I believe it was worth it.

Most employees in Australia are entitled to long service leave if they have been working for the same employer for an extended period of time. Long service leave typically accumulates after 10 years, and entitles you to two months of paid leave. But the entitlement is different depending on the source of your long service leave entitlement. You can look up the National Employment Standards (NES) contained in the *Fair Work Act 2009* for more information.

Whether you're on holidays or taking long service leave, don't miss the opportunity to restructure your household finances while you take time off work.

Leave the financial baggage at home

Planning your finances in preparation for the break can be enlightening. The greatest benefit will be that you'll travel light. By this I mean your financial baggage — the weight upon your shoulders — will be eased. Equally, as you face the return from your break, you can take comfort in knowing that you haven't left (too many) loose ends that will trip you up upon your return. You will know or at least have estimated how much money you are going to spend and have spent, and how much you will need when you get home, allowing you to thoroughly enjoy your break.

And of course, if you aren't much of a planner, I suggest you don't lose sight of the simple 'Stop, Start, Continue' process from earlier in the chapter. It could save you mega bill shocks.

Take time to:

◆ reflect on your success

◆ reconsider what matters most to you

◆ reconnect with your personal money values (chapter 2)

◆ ensure your wealth purpose is clear

◆ take some financial advice (if you haven't already)

◆ invest in your personal finance village (chapter 4)

◆ do your next one- to five-year plan (see the following activity).

Make a one- to five-year financial plan

I worked with a wonderful executive coach by the name of Joy Pitts, who shared this activity with me 15 years ago and I still use it to this day. If you have a partner, sit down and do this at the same time as they do and then share the details of your thoughts when you've finished.

CHECK THE REAR VIEW

- When you look back over the past 12 months, what was your greatest success?

- What did you learn about yourself from this experience?

- What was your greatest disappointment this past year?

- What did you learn from this experience?

- In the context of your whole life, what was a theme or metaphor that might aptly describe your overall experience last year?

LOOK FORWARD

- When you look forward, what is your biggest dream (or goal) for the next one to five years? (If it doesn't make you gulp or get your heart pumping, you might not be stretching yourself enough.)

- What would achieving this bring into your life?

- Which of your values does it honour?

- Who will you need to become (i.e. what type of person) to successfully accomplish your dream?

- What are the beliefs or behaviours you will need to let go of to become that person?

- What are the beliefs or behaviours that will assist you in moving ahead?

- From the perspective of your whole life journey, what do you want this next year to be about?

START PLANNING

- List the specific actions you will need to take to successfully initiate your journey towards your purpose or future vision.

- List the support you will need to keep the focus and make the changes required to accomplish your purpose/future vision.

(continued)

- What might get in the way of you achieving these actions?

- When and how will you start moving towards this?

- Write down your key actions for next year with time frames.

Don't forget to discuss your goals with your partner.

Did you discover that you would like to see a break or even a sabbatical on your five-year horizon? I certainly hope so. There's one on mine!

Stop worrying now

1. Is it time for you to consider a break of some kind? If so, what's the next step you can take to make this a reality? (Maybe the first step is to give yourself permission to *stop* and then consider what's possible.)

2. Next, plan a four-day weekend to allow yourself the time to dream or make a plan. Schedule some long weekends into your diary right now to enable adequate planning time.

3. Is there a special project at home, a course you wanted to study or a hobby that needs some dedicated time from you? Or perhaps a holiday in Italy or Greece? A road trip around Australia? A new business venture? Give some thought to what you might like to do if you have a planned break.

Chapter 11

Set up a side hustle or business successfully

On the one hand, thinking about how to create additional sources of income can be a dynamic and engaging experience; on the other hand it could create more for you to worry about. So, with this in mind it is important to consider this chapter in the context of what's possible and what might be in your goals. Not everyone will want to set up a side hustle or business — nor should everyone.

When you worry about money it's likely you'll also think about how you can make more of it (and I don't mean planning a heist)! Creating optionality in your income earning stream by setting up a business or side hustle might create the extra cash you're looking for.

How you decide if it's a good idea and if it will alleviate your worries comes down to planning and keeping your eyes wide open to make sure it doesn't become the stuff nightmares are made of.

If you're reading this as an existing business owner, I'm sure you're aware that there are plenty of potholes along the way — and good for you if you've missed stepping in any. It also won't hurt to take a fresh look at your business: how it's serving you and whether things need a bit of a change.

Considering your options

Earlier in my career, I had a long-term contract with a recruitment company that had a line of business called outplacement. Outplacement is a service that helps people navigate change, sometimes after redundancy, or to find a new job. It's also a process that helps work out what matters to you about your career and what you value.

I was lucky enough to be at the end of the line — or perhaps the beginning, depending on how you looked at it. When the outplacement agency referred people to me, they were typically frustrated, burnt-out executives, deeply worried about retaining their income, taking a pause, disillusioned with the corporate lives they no longer wanted to pursue and often considering starting their own business.

Could this be you?

Maybe you grew up in a family business. Maybe it's the only way you know how to make money. Maybe you need to supplement or replace your income (to find a way to provide greater financial security). Or maybe you've ground to a halt as a salary employee and want to break out...

It's usual to feel terrified of leaving the job security of a salary. But it's equally worrying staying tied to a job that you're unhappy in.

There are so many valid reasons for wanting to set up your own business, whether that's to work in it full time, part time or as something on the side while you raise your kids (mums *and* dads included).

In fact, there are approximately 2.5 million small businesses in Australia. Yet unfortunately, 20 per cent of new businesses in Australia fail each year and up to 60 per cent of start-ups will not survive beyond five years of launching.

I'm not sharing these statistics to make you worry more. Turning your mind to starting your own business or side hustle (or both) can be life changing, as it was for me. Owning a successful business is terrific and rewarding, but you also need to know and plan for the realities as these can be different from your expectations.

How you plan and execute on your business plan will be the difference between your basic survival and long-term success.

Don't start with the sexy stuff, start with *why*

I've navigated this well-trodden path for myself and clients for 30 years and I know it's not straight forward and it's not for everyone.

So it's important to understand *why* you are considering starting a business and what has led you to this point, first up. My goal is to ensure you transition into this new environment having considered your options well. You need to be clear on your motivation for starting your business. Assuming you know what the business is or will be, it's great to share this with a trusted advisor from your personal finance village, or maybe close family, to test the robustness of your thinking.

I can't emphasise enough how much planning is required when going about your new business. To an onlooker it might look easier than it is.

Most people want to start with the sexy stuff, like:

- creating your business plan
- naming your business
- designing the brand
- working out what technology you might need
- developing a website
- estimating what additional capital you might need
- choosing where to work from
- hiring people to help.

Put the effort into considering what life as a self-employed person might actually look like.

A business can add to your money worries exponentially, so doing your research and having realistic expectations about the skills and effort (that is, your focused time) required will go a long way to helping you nail it.

You may be over the chained-to-the-desk, 40-hour week, and taking direction from someone else in your executive job. But that's about the equivalent of working Monday to Wednesday in your own business — and then you'll likely have another 40 hours of work from Thursday to Saturday! Nine times out of 10 people underestimate what is required. I'd say it's all-consuming in a good way if you're passionate about it. If you're not passionate about it, it's the *wrong* business and it's wrong for you to consider heading down this path.

A simple pros and cons list is a good way to start. I've given you some examples to start with and space to add your own.

Pros	Cons
Earning independent income	*Not sure I can afford to stop earning my regular income*
Being my own boss	*Lumpy income*

Pros	Cons
Potential to make more money	Having to make all the decisions
Making all the decisions	I might have to work all the time
Flexibility to work whenever I want	I don't understand accounting or cash flows
Learning new skills such as bookkeeping, marketing or business development	I've never been good at marketing
Choosing who I work with	I have to work up a business plan (this is time consuming too)
I've got a great business idea to explore	I may need to understand how intellectual property laws work
What I build I can keep or, even better, sell	I'll need to be self-motivated

Where to start?

One of the greatest experiences I've had is working with start-up hubs. If you're not familiar with these, they are usually a workspace where many (and typically new) business owners come together under one roof using shared services such as web development, office space, mentoring or even funding to get their businesses going. I'm sure there is one near you. It's a business model in itself and it might help you get going with your business more quickly.

My role in the start-up hubs is to provide business advice and coaching to the entrepreneurs as part of their village when they kick off their new businesses. In many cases these businesses were side hustles that they had big plans for. You could say that most businesses begin looking like a start-up, and there is a lot we can learn from these founders. Perhaps the main difference is that they tend to want to scale quickly. The purpose of scaling quickly is to attract investors, which in turn means cash/capital to rapidly facilitate the growth plans of the business so they can possibly sell or list their business on a stock exchange as a way to exit the business. This is one option for you to consider.

The reason these businesses were often a side hustle is because these people still had day jobs. They kept their day job because they needed to earn income to put food on the table and pay their rent (or mortgage) while they got their new business up and running. Working their day job was really a means to an end — let's call it financial survival. People often performed a normal work week and worked on their side hustle after hours and weekends, usually until it would bust them with exhaustion, or they were able to raise capital to help run and expand the business to give them some breathing space and a small income. Start-ups can test you in ways you never imagined. Right from the get-go.

Start-up hubs can be brilliant spaces to find like-minded people and add to your network. You might also locate others to add to your village who can help too. It's not all fancy offices either. Rubbing shoulders with people in this way helps you work out what you need and learn the realities of what it's like setting up and running a business.

Have you got hidden lazy money?

Have you heard of a *lazy balance sheet*? It's a term accountants use when they know their clients have assets sitting on their balance sheet that aren't generating income or are generating a low return.

If you've decided to buy yourself a lifestyle property, a little getaway or you've purchased a caravan to take a few holidays in, consider these your next side hustle. Why have them sit unused, collecting dust for periods of time, when you could have them listed on Airbnb, Stayz or

Camplify and earn extra cash to supplement your income? Sure, you might not want to share your place with anyone (and that's a trade-off), and getting it organised will require a bit of extra work, but it could close the gap in your money worries.

Leaving them sitting idly does enforce the lazy balance sheet and when you consider that money could be generating an income stream for you, it's hard to ignore.

If you're put off by the whole process or simply don't have the time, why not consider engaging an Airbnb manager? You can pay them to do it for you. There are plenty of people renting out their homes who are time poor and will happily pay others to manage their property (and do the cleaning) for them.

The rising cost of living and real wages not increasing is giving people incentive to develop extra income from side hustles in this way. Bringing in a few extra dollars helps reduce the worry created by the growing gap between income and costs. Many people report that this also provides some relief from the mental load of their day job.

Join the gig economy

ABS data shows that over 6.5 per cent of Aussies have a second job. Thanks to the gig economy, there are some easy ways to get this going too, with minimal stress and limited set-up costs. It's easy to offer your time or services via one of the community platforms (or job marketplaces) such as Airtasker, TaskRabbit, Fiverr or Freelancer, just to name a few. And if it's pure cash you're looking for, you can offer your time in a different way, such as a ridesharing service as a driver, fast-food delivery, dog walking services—there are even people looking for someone to put their rubbish bins out every week! It's a bonus if you find that you're doing something you love and you'll always find time for it.

A side hustle can be really simple. It could also be the catalyst or segue to developing a more substantial business over time.

New business, new worries?

If you have the desire to set up a business, or are already running one, then it's important to check in on the realities of running it.

Take a look at these top tips for remedies to prevent business failure.

1. *Do your research.* You need to understand the market need for your product or service. Are you sure there is a need? Can you identify any similar products or any trends in the industry you are entering? Do you know who your competitors are (understand what they do well, or maybe where the gaps might be)? Who are you targeting? How will you grab their attention? What is the hook to get them to work with you?

2. *Create a living business plan.* My pet peeve is people going to the trouble of creating a business plan and then putting it in a drawer and never looking at it again! Make it count. It will help set your direction and an action plan for your business goals and objectives. Be organised about it. You know what they say: 'Failing to plan is planning to fail!' A plan will help you focus and stay on track (especially if you revisit it regularly).

3. *Get the financial support or backing you need.* Your business plan will go part of the way to securing the cash you need to start your business. You have to be clear on what costs are required to set up and run your business. Set-up costs often come as a shock. Consider whether you need to borrow money. Business loans can be expensive, so you might need to finance equipment instead of buying it outright to balance or smooth cash needs in your first six months.

4. *Manage cash flow like your life depends on it.* Follow the golden rule: 'cash is king'. It's so important to make sure that you are being paid on a similar timeline to when you pay your suppliers, so look carefully at the payment terms. Marry income with outgoings as well as possible. How is the business bank balance?

Are your debtors paying you in a timely manner? Are you ensuring you pay your creditors on time?

5. *Become a marketing ace or work with someone who is.* Marketing your business is a necessary and ongoing requirement to continue to have visitors or customers come to your business or visit your website. It's also critical for attracting new customers and for retaining your loyal customers. I'm sure you like it when a product you have used and are loyal to posts on Instagram and shares a new model or improved version. Or the people running the local eatery add something new to the menu, giving you another reason to pop by.

    There are many options for marketing both online and offline. Remember to measure your return on investment so you know what channel or marketing tool works for you. (For example, has there been an increase in visitors to your business or website since you did a local area mail drop?) Have you considered the role of an influencer in your marketing strategy?

6. *Stay on top of customer needs and your competition.* Asking for feedback is one of the most powerful ways to stay on top of your customers' needs. Don't be afraid to seek feedback: it's a gift. You can build greater loyalty by taking this feedback on board. Needs change over time, but don't lose sight of your customers once you are knee deep in running your business. Losing sight of them can have people running to your competition. If possible, develop a healthy relationship with your competitors. I like to think the world is big enough for everyone.

7. *Learn to love change.* You are bound to face challenges along the way in your business, so it would be wise to remember the motto 'failing cheaply and quickly' rather than hanging on. Don't be afraid to call it. Equally, welcome change for you, for your industry and for your customer. Embrace change and ensure your business is responding to it. Being adaptable impacts business longevity.

8. *Be clear about the pace of growth that works for you.* Ever heard of growing pains? It's a balancing act starting a business and with all of your pre-work done so well, sometimes your business can feel like a runaway success, but being prepared for future growth is an important success factor. Consider what the growing needs could be in your business, such as the number of people you need, type of technology, working space, greater customer expectations, new industry regulations. Growth can be a major business risk and you need to create a plan that can address it.

9. *Recruit and retain the right people.* When starting out, consider who you need to close your skill gap. Who do you need to hire to complement your skills? Then consider diversity, personal fit, attitude and experience. The next challenge is retaining people and working to create a culture that makes people want to stay. Even better is if they hear about how good your culture is from their peer groups who work for your competitors and want to join your business!

10. *Seek help and support.* As I mentioned at the start of the chapter, your own business can be extremely rewarding, but exhaustion can also destroy you and the business. Being an entrepreneur can be lonely. You must reach out to your peers, have a coffee with them, listen to a business-minded podcast, locate a business coach and talk to your accountant. They can all help you. Dialling up your personal finance village *early* is a must. Talking regularly to your trusted advisor about the health of your business will go a long way towards keeping you focused.

Setting you up for financial success

Financial ~~mis~~management is arguably the main determinant in business success. Money stress can plague business owners who don't have their hands on the till, so to speak. You'll need a laser focus on cash flow. Being across your daily and weekly sales in detail is a good starting point, followed closely by understanding the outgoings of your business and estimating future costs such as tax. Too often business owners confess that they don't have enough money to pay their tax bill.

When you run a business, and you estimate that your total business income (turnover) will be in excess of $75000 during a year, you need to charge GST (goods and services tax) on top of what you would price your products or services at. This 10 per cent belongs to the government so you have to pass it on to the ATO (Australian Taxation Office).

Your Business Activity Statement (BAS) is generally required to be lodged and paid with the ATO every quarter depending on your business turnover. Three months can fly buy in a business, especially a new one. Money comes in, money gets spent and before you know it, it's time to lodge your BAS. To stay on track, you need to plan and prepare your cash flows for this.

There are three main things to consider in your financial management of the business:

1. *Get your GST right.* Set aside 10 per cent of what you collect, so that when you need to pay your GST, it's there. Of course, you get to offset the 10 per cent of products or services that you have paid for in your business, although, if you have a higher turnover it's more likely that you will be paying GST to the ATO.

2. *Set aside a percentage of your profit so you can pay your tax.* I was sitting at lunch with friends not long ago and they were complaining about their upcoming tax bill, to which I replied, 'Hey, paying tax is a good thing — at least you know you've made money.'

   The good news is, you only have to pay tax if you make a profit. The trick is to ensure you set aside money for your business taxes as you go and so you don't spend all your profit and then get a big surprise. Ensure that before you go and spend all your profit you set aside a percentage for tax.

Having said that, one of the greatest advantages of the Australian pay-as-you-go system is that you really shouldn't end up too far behind. (Just make sure you sign up to it to help you stay on top of your taxes.) Invariably, a lot can change in a quarter and people get caught short. Don't let that be you.

3. *Make sure you invest in a business software package to account for your sales and expenses.* It will make your life so much easier and serve you better than an Excel spreadsheet (or scraps of paper that you call receipts!). There is also a cascading effect with your accountant. If you are engaging them to help you, it's likely to save you dollars in the end if you are recording details in a software package. Examples of business accounting software packages include Xero (from as little as $14.50 per month and you don't have to be an accountant to use it), MYOB and QuickBooks.

Choose your business structure early to reduce worry

In Australia, there are four types of business structure to choose from and choosing early is likely to reduce additional work and worry down the track should you find you have to change the structure because you didn't get it right in the first place.

Thorough planning when you start will reduce the need to change the structure and help avoid unnecessary costs for new advice. It's important to understand each option before you get advice on making a decision. Accountants and/or tax advisors are best placed to give you advice on the most suitable business structure. When you speak to them, make sure you give them all the facts about the business. Explain your current vision, so that they consider the right structure for now that will carry you into the future.

My advice is two-fold: make sure you engage a professional *up front* (most likely a new addition to your personal finance village, such as an accountant, tax advisor or lawyer) *and* start simple (that is, as a sole trader). If there are two or more of you who 'own' the business (that is, co-founders) you might consider a partnership. Partnerships are just what the word suggests: a partnership for two or more business owners. They are risky beasts though because you are jointly and severally liable for everything your business partner does (that should scare you off). For example, they could run off with the bank balance!

Here's a high-level explanation of each of the options for structuring a business. Note how they each come with different responsibilities.

	Advantages	Disadvantages
Sole trader	Simple, cheap to set up You can pay employees, just not yourself Responsible for your own super	Lack of asset protection — if it goes bad, you are at risk of losing all of your assets
Partnership	Inexpensive to set up Needs a partnership agreement (to agree on how income and losses are shared) Doesn't pay tax because it's shared to the partners and they then pay tax	Lack of asset protection Joint and several liability for each partner's actions — that is, if your partner does something wrong, your assets are exposed
Company	Run by directors and owned by shareholders Regulated by ASIC (Australian Securities and Investments Commission) Pays tax based on profit More commercially accepted Limits your liability Fixed tax rate	Higher set-up costs and administration More reporting obligations Less flexibility
Trust	Needs a trustee to be legally responsible for the trust (can be an individual — such as yourself — or a company) Profit gets distributed out to the beneficiaries, who pay the tax Greatest flexibility for profit	Most expensive to set up because you need a trust deed to explain how it operates Less commercially accepted as a business vehicle so harder to work with

As we've touched on, structure choice is a key part of the process in setting up your business because a poor structure could cost you dearly down the track (for example, in taxes). It's a lot to think about when you are just getting your head around all the complexities or new things you haven't done before. If you expect to grow your business (most likely) or you're taking on a new business partner or even thinking you may sell the business down the track, your choice of structure is a critical decision.

Begin with the end in mind! Take this opportunity to refresh your personal financial village and ensure you're surrounded by realistic advisors who will keep you engaged and focused on your business goals.

Stop worrying now

1. If you commit to starting your side hustle or business, what are the trade-offs that you need to consider in making this decision?

2. Take a moment to jot down your business idea/s.

3. Can you determine what the business might add to your income and what type of revenue you could generate from it?

4. How would running your own business make you feel?

5. Who would you need (to hire and add to your personal finance village) to help you on this journey?

6. What are your *next three steps* to starting your worry-free business journey?

Chapter 12

Consider a sea-change, tree-change or move

Over the past few years, there's been an unprecedented shift in how we work and where we live in Australia. We have been relocating our families to the coast or the country in increasing numbers, and rethinking our lives: how can we reduce the noise and costs and lead happier and more fulfilling lives?

There's no doubt there continues to be growing demand for living outside a main city. The Regional Movers Index shows that the trend for migration from the city to regional towns is likely to continue. There's no doubt that the sheer level of net migration during the 2020 pandemic represented a steep change in the overall size of many regional communities. This trend continues to be well ahead of pre-2020 levels, albeit at a less aggressive pace, so hopefully this is giving many regional communities some breathing space to adjust.

The 2023 McGrath Report on property trends also suggests that the rise in house prices for our regional coastal areas is forcing the city escapees to choose the bush over the beach when they relocate. Couple this trend with financial constraints on big-city housing affordability and our rising cost of living and a sea-change or a tree-change (now referred to as a sea-tree change) could be the cure for your money worries.

Many of us are making decisions about where we want to live and be happy, and that's often because of the financial implications. Start with the fundamentals. Why pay $1.5 million for an inner-city property when you could pay half that amount and have money left over for investing (to build a passive income stream — yippee!) to create genuine financial security (win, win, win!).

Let's face it, inner-city living has its downsides and is well known for being taxing on your cost of living. There is noise, less space, it can be difficult to park and crime is statistically higher. You can see how this is impacting moves away from the city. Along with the greater options available to continue your city career out of town, it's a no-brainer.

When you consider these issues and all of the possible life stages we go through — such as marriage/births/retirement/sickness/career change/job change/relationship breakdown and the impact that living in a big city can have on us — it's no surprise that Millennials are leading the net migration to the regions. Millennials are those aged between 24 and 40 years, and they are followed closely by Gen Alpha and Gen Z (24 and under at the time of writing). Where you see the cost of living amplified in Australia's biggest cities such as Sydney and Melbourne the exodus is bigger.

Is it time for a change?

There are lots of triggers for people considering a move. (Before we completely launch into your move *out* of the city, some of you might be considering a move *to* the city or to another place. If that's you, skip ahead to the section 'Before you up and move'.)

There are individual triggers: some people are simply looking for a change; others are fed up with commuting and want more affordable space around them, or are sick of the bills.

People also want a sense of community and may not be feeling it in the city but recognise the country is renowned for a strong sense of kinship. Most people seem to make the call to move out of the city when they have young children (the statistics demonstrate this) so they can get them into schools and immersed in country life before they reach their teenage years.

At the other end of the age spectrum, a move to the country helps fast-track plans towards retirement by signalling to the world that you are changing pace.

Here's a more in-depth list of why people consider making a move from the city. Which ones apply to you?

- ☐ 'I feel overburdened by the city cost of living and worry how I will keep up longer term.'

- ☐ 'I'm currently pursuing alternative employment opportunities (changing jobs, approaching retirement, facing redundancy or moving location).'

- ☐ 'I've already achieved a level of success in my professional life and am wondering "what next?"'

- ☐ 'I have a long-held dream I'd love to pursue, and I feel like now is the time to realise it.'

- ☐ 'The reasons I moved to a city don't seem to exist any more.'

- ☐ 'I feel burnt out by the relentlessness of city life: long hours, endless commuting, stress and a poor work–life balance with precious little time to be with those I love, doing what I love.'

- ☐ 'My current job is boring, predictable, lacks challenge and is often frustrating. I feel like it's past its use-by date.'

- ☐ 'I love the thought of doing something that matters — a simpler and more fulfilling life by the sea, in the country, working from home.'

- [ ] 'I find it hard sometimes to catch a breath when we are so busy living our city life and it feels a little out of control, especially from a cost perspective. Costs just keep rising and everything we do seems expensive.'

- [ ] 'I believe the country offers a more wholesome lifestyle option than the city.'

Even if you've ticked some, or many, of these, it's important to note it doesn't necessarily mean you're ready to move.

Before you start making announcements and informing your work colleagues that you're going to ditch the grind, you need to do your due diligence about what a move like this actually entails.

It's just like starting a new business. You need to know the ins and outs of this move *before* you do it. While the fresh air beckons you, give yourself some time to make sure you aren't purely focused on all the well-documented upsides of country living. Be sure to go in with your eyes wide open on the potential downsides too. You want to test this to ensure that your overarching financial goals and wellbeing are intact long after you have settled into your new lifestyle.

We know there are many pluses about living away from the city, but the reality can be something else — for example, small-town infrastructure is not built for the masses; it might be hard to get in to see a GP; or there may be only *one* small local school. Some people made moves during the pandemic only to return to the city after lockdowns to get stronger internet connectivity and to get back to bigger, 'proper' schools for their kids.

It needs to be right for you!

When you're doing your due diligence, it's key to keep checking back on your motivations. If, like many people, you want to stop worrying about money and you see a move out of the city as giving you the much-needed cost relief and shot in the arm for your financial future, make sure you plan to ensure success!

City versus country

Country life seems simpler, and it appears easier to spend less in the country than it does in the city. There are fewer shopping options and fewer services, but this doesn't mean it's not wonderful. There's no doubt a move out of the city will have you smashing your savings goals more quickly than would be possible in the city. This is the first thing my friends who have moved out of the city recognise.

The sheer pleasure of locally made sourdough bread, your own free-range eggs, and herbs and vegetables straight from the garden — you eat whatever is in season. There are farmers' markets where you can buy fresh produce rather than buying it from the IGA store. Your protein sources are locally farmed. Your butcher might only sell local product. There is space around you — blank space sometimes too. It gets dark, really dark, at night because there aren't any lights around (unless you made the sea-tree change to a main street, of course). You can have a hills hoist (my favourite) with fresh air to blow dry your clothes. Electricity: another big saving!

If you have kids, they might put away their screens more often. You will make compromises on catching up with family if they are back in the city, but better still you might now have space for them to visit you! You might find the local community is a lot stronger and possibly more vocal than your city one, and more passionate about change. Even more progressive or more polarised. The Facebook group will share information about the height of the creek crossing, cattle on a local road, a broken fence and the location of tradespeople — in contrast to council feedback and who keeps leaving dog poop on the nature strip peppering your city neighbourhood page.

I've painted a pretty awesome picture of a sea-tree change, haven't I? Sounds idyllic? What's not to love: saving money, building your path to financial freedom, reducing your cost of living, becoming healthier and happier?

Let me balance this with ensuring you are aware of some of the downsides and financial costs of regional living.

Our regions are challenged for resources, and this will impact you. If you think there is a resource issue in the city, it has a multiplier effect in the regions.

Hospitals don't have all the x-ray equipment. They have a general doctor and few specialists, and if you get really sick you will (most likely) need to commute to the city or a bigger regional area for medical support. Travelling for medical treatment comes with a cost. Roads don't get the same level of attention as the ones in the city so they are rough. And your small, zippy city car might need to be upgraded to better suit the road conditions. You might find internet is expensive because you need satellite. If you buy a fixerupperer and you plan to renovate with local assistance, be aware of what is available — people constantly get let down that the services aren't the same as in the city and maybe you will be delayed longer than expected. Or worse, you will pay for someone to commute to you from a city (charging double due to the travel time). Smaller towns, smaller networks, everyone knows something about someone, and the bush telegraph can be painful. And you might find the peace and quiet awful!

> **You begin to see, like all change, the pendulum might swing one way for you and at the same time take a big swing back. The realities of your move may not be immediately obvious, so you need to be clear on everything this involves.**

Before you up and move

Setting a timeline up front for when you plan to move and how long you intend to move for (for example, permanent, five years, not sure) will help you identify clearer financial goals or outcomes. Don't forget, the move might be for a good time, and doesn't need to be for a long time. It depends on what is right for you.

Take a look at these tips and potential traps for your sea-tree change. Each tip is designed to reduce your worry, get you clear on the financial implications of the move and in equal measure act as risk mitigation for your plan.

Tips	Traps
Spend time in the region before you buy	Buying without spending time to research, rushing in
Try summer and winter seasons	Only trying one season and not experiencing the extremes, which you may find you dislike
Renting initially may give you a good insight into the place you are choosing	Renting options may be more limited so expect this to take longer
Prepare a revised 'open your front door' expenses list (see chapter 1) Information is power, so make sure you know the costs	Getting caught up in the euphoria and failing to update your costs will expose you to money worries once you've settled
Prepare a new baseline (see chapter 1)	Lack of awareness of your baseline costs will have you off track when it comes to your financial goals
Reset your financial goals with meaningful outcomes aligned to your sea-tree change — that is, save a greater percentage of your income, and invest the proceeds of the sale from your city home (see chapter 2)	No plan, no upside. If you don't reset your goals, you are likely to meander and not achieve longer term financial security
Check out childcare options and their costs	Childcare may not available
Acreage comes with maintenance: recognise that if you end up with half an acre or more around you it will need more maintenance than your city pad	Not budgeting maintenance for large land area (e.g. weeds and grass)

(continued)

Tips	Traps
Renovating can add value to your house, if this is part of your plan Consider the budget implications (is more dollars aligned to your financial goals?)	Understand what trades are available. These can be limited in regional areas, and you might get caught out (e.g. tradies may need to travel to get to you and charge you extra)
Confirm the source, speed and cost of internet: in some regional areas it relies on satellite such as Starlink, which comes at a $3000 installation and set-up cost	Not checking the internet service, speed and price. You might be significantly delayed in settling without it (e.g. you can't start working), or you might need to rent an office in the main town that has internet (people often have to do this, and it's an additional cost)
Join the local Facebook group	Joining a local debate on Facebook
Spend time at the local pub. It's likely to have good pub meals, a great source of local information (or gossip), a new network and clarity about the local vibe	Ignoring the locals will have you out of the loop permanently
Understand the local job market. This is important if you're considering a career change as well	Not recognising that the job market is different
Know transport alternatives in and out of your town, such as rail or bus services that will impact your travel costs	Assuming you will only drive
Check and understand education options	Not recognising the limited options without travel
Understand available health services and if there is a service you use regularly in the city, check whether it exists in the region	Travelling for medical reasons can also add significant expense to your baseline costs
Find new friends (park run/arts and culture events/volunteer locally/ men's shed and CWA)	Keeping to yourself
Stay connected with family and so you don't end up a mess trying to juggle returning to the city, look for options such as meeting mid-way or a family retreat to catch up	Always heading back to the city to visit (time and cost impacts)
Maximise your commute time: call family to check in (see above point), learn a new language, listen to your favourite music, download before you go, get your podcasts organised)	Unplanned long commutes

Tips	Traps
Buy noise-cancelling earphones for public transport and a battery back-up for your phone	Forgetting your earphones and charger

The more you plan and test your objectives, the more likely you are to stop worrying about money.

Prepare a cost-of-living comparison

An essential step for you to successfully move is to compare your soon-to-be-old life baseline costs with your sea-tree change life costs. The easiest way is to initially estimate as well as you can using like-for-like comparisons. Note my earlier tip: if you are unsure about a cost in your new location, drop a note on the Facebook page. You'll more than likely find locals are quick to respond with guidance.

To help walk you through how to do this, let's look at a hypothetical example.

Romy and John: a sea-tree change

For a long time, Romy and John had been considering a move. They had been cramped into a three-bedroom apartment, raising their kids. The kids shared rooms to create better working space for them all. They had really outgrown this space, but appreciated the proximity to everything including their work. Access to suitable housing within their budget was a big consideration for Romy and John in making a move.

The kids were still in primary school so now was the best time to take this leap. They had increased flexibility with working from home (they just needed the space to do it) and knew they could compromise on the commute for a day or two per week if that

(continued)

was essential for their work. It was important for them to make the move before the kids reached high school, as they hoped this would make it easier for the kids to settle in.

The whole family had spent many family holidays along the coastline so you could say they had done their reconnaissance over an extensive period of time, slowly collating their list of likes and dislikes for the places they chose to holiday at and beginning to narrow down their choices for a forever home in the country. The final decision was to find a home within the 2.5-hour radius of the city, where they would have space and good proximity to schools and other services, could access beaches and the bush, and an important factor was that the road to the city (preferably a freeway) was readily accessible from the place they chose. A bonus would be a trainline close to the location of their forever home, so they would have more than one option for returning to the city.

The decision to sea-tree change had been tedious for Romy and John. It was now or never after many ponderings. The financial choice to move was the biggest motivator—at least, they had expected this to have the single greatest impact for them. They wanted to retain the lifestyle they had in the city but in the rural kind of way (without compromising their savings). It wasn't so much about Uber Eats (which didn't exist where they were heading) but about healthy living, country air, more outdoor activities, space and a slower pace.

They filled out a 'compare and contrast financial comparison' to cement their commitment to the move.

You can create the same table for yourself, and insert your costs to assess whether you are better off financially from the move before it's too late for you to slow the process down and you feel committed—that is, before you've sold your city house and booked the kids into a new school.

'Open your *new* front door' and baseline variations	Pre move (old life)	Post move (new life)	Cost impact (+ or −)	Your net cost impact ($)
Baseline from chapter 1				
Moving costs (year 1 cost only): moving can be expensive; investigate options for doing it yourself vs a removalist			+ (plus additional cost)	
Power	Electricity bill	Solar and off-grid option	− (less reduction in cost)	
Internet connection (additional cost for year 1 only)	City price	Same as city or additional infrastructure required (most likely)	+	
Internet usage	City price	Change as different provider required	+	
Transport (still need two cars)	Petrol and parking fees	Petrol and rail combo (no parking fees)	+	
Groceries	By all your groceries	Grow your own vegetables and use your own chook eggs	−	
Mortgage (depends on price of upgrade — assume you are upsizing)		Note — by contrast a CBD upgrade would have been a massive financial hit	−	

(continued)

'Open your new front door' and baseline variations	Pre move (old life)	Post move (new life)	Cost impact (+ or −)	Your net cost impact ($)
Or rent option			−	
Lifestyle — more cooking at home	More eating out	Less eating out	−	
Lifestyle	Lots of conveniences	Fewer conveniences	−	
Lifestyle	Likely to use Uber Eats and Uber drivers	No Uber Eats, Uber drivers, etc.	−	
Lifestyle	shopping or browsing more likely	Less discretionary spending, less shopping or browsing without purpose	−	
Health and beauty	Gym, beauty	No gym, no manicure	−	
Net cost (benefit to move)			Net reduction in baseline costs	

For Romy and John, the impact of the increased mortgage was significant but far less significant than any move they would have planned in the city. It has given them greater flexibility to create a version of financial freedom where they can see the choice to move positively impacting their ability to create meaningful financial goals that marry with their lifestyle choices.

Given they had not 'lived' out of the city, they decided to pack up their place and rent something in the region they liked (this is a great strategy, in my view). This was really a test although their intention was not to return. This also opened up some options for them in terms of location. They were able to rent their apartment in the city, which helped cover the mortgage and a share of their new rental. They took a six-month lease, a wise investment into their future home. Weekends were spent combing the backroads and attending inspections to narrow their search.

Roll forward a year, and the city apartment is sold. Romy, John and the kids have settled into a lovely two-acre property bursting with space and a rambling cottage 'that needs work' with a room for each of them. It sounds idyllic and that's just what it is. They had long wanted to escape the hustle and bustle of the city and that's exactly what they had found. They are close to wildlife with bird sounds in abundance, and their early evenings are shaped by roo and wallaby spotting. Wildlife seems to be everywhere! Their neighbours have a horse and others around them have small hobby-type farms with all manner of animals including ducks, alpacas and sheep. They have four chickens that lay eggs most days. A veggie patch is also taking shape and plans for some additions are in the wings.

Taking the step towards a sea-tree change creates the circumstances to enable a financial reset for your family. But achieving this reset requires planning.

Once you have undertaken a compare-and-contrast analysis, you'll know the key changes to your budget. This will in turn create additional savings opportunities for you to consider, which may improve your overall financial health.

Be healthy, wealthy and wise

Sometimes simply (re)framing our worries is all it takes to dislodge stubborn, long-held thinking. It's possible that a sea-tree change will be the catalyst for you to reset and start to secure your financial future. It represents a great opportunity to develop new, practical, within-reach financial goals.

Of course, there are plenty of things to consider in looking at a move away from the city and you need to make sure it's right for you and your family.

Open space, peace and quiet, clean air and a whole lot less stuff! Research from the Australian Unity Wellbeing Index and Deakin University demonstrates that living in the country is beneficial for both your physical and mental health and we have demonstrated that it's good for your balance sheet and financial future as well.

Make sure you take the opportunity to make the change a positive step for your wealth. For example, when going for a like-for-like accommodation option with their sea-tree change, most people find that if they are coming from renting in the city to buying in the region and taking on a mortgage, they are far better off financially. By contrast, if you decide to upsize your mortgage, the financial benefit of a move is lost.

Is a move away from the city more about a complete shift in your lifestyle?

Over time you might also consider whether you need to continue with your city job at all. You might investigate an option closer to your new place of abode. For some people, relocating to a business with an office closer to their nearest regional centre might make more sense. And always investigate job relocation options that might exist if you are part of a bigger business. Employers may offer relocation allowances, which would help with your move costs or even your stamp duty.

We know that earning more money generally means you spend more (remember income and expense creep from chapter 1). A sea-tree change may be the alternative to the burdensome costs of your lifestyle that can only be changed by you.

The regions are full of entrepreneurs making a simpler living: making the choice to recycle, reuse, live off the land, and conscious choices to spend less and simply live off less.

Just make sure you weigh up all the options before you make a big move.

Stop worrying now

Follow this checklist to make sure you do your due diligence *before* you make a big move or exodus from your current home:

1. Spend time at the proposed location (have a holiday or two there).

2. Get to understand the housing market (this is critical to determine the likely cost in housing changeover). Note: as Romy and John were upsizing, they wanted to set a clear ceiling in terms of the price they were prepared to pay to move, recognising that they wanted this to be their forever home so they considered what was a fair increase to take on, while a longer term comparative saving would be the case due to the price of regional vs city real estate.

3. Understand the proximity of schools and services you need in the area.

4. Consider the job market for future reference.

5. Look into the overall financial impact of the change you are considering.

6. Prepare a cost-of-living comparison.

7. Reset your financial goals.

Chapter 13
Give and gift to causes bigger than yourself

You've spent the last 12 chapters investing in yourself, curing your own money worries. Let's also remember that there is always someone in a worse position than you. Over the years I have learned and experienced that taking the focus off myself — facing things outwards, instead of being inward with money worries — can actually be a great way of dealing with these worries.

Maybe now it's time for you to help someone else worry less about their struggles. Lending a hand by giving your time or money can have such a significant impact for both you as the giver and for the recipient. The happiness you will experience by giving will surpass any sacrifice, however big or small, to you. There are powerful lessons to be learned from giving: it can be contagious, it bolsters feelings of gratitude, it helps with social connection and it's good for your health.

*It's easy to whirlpool into despair
when you feel your money worries are
insurmountable, but the therapy gained
from giving might be just the ticket to
pull you out.*

Remember, giving is not solely about money. Giving comes in many shapes and forms. You have the freedom to give, when it's right for you. How much, is up to you.

Humpty Dumpty Foundation (HDF)

Let's look at one ordinary person's giving journey that spans 30 years.

Paul Francis: giving back

Paul Francis had a varied career. He worked in the insurance industry after leaving school, then in the manufacturing and retailing of tennis gear. He had always had an interest in tennis as his parents ran a tennis centre when he was growing up, although they didn't want him to be in the tennis business. He eventually kicked off his tennis coaching career after a few twists and turns and ran a coaching business.

While he was courtside one day, Paul decided it was time to give back to the community. He really wanted to help others. Royal North Shore Hospital (RNSH) was nearby, and he thought raising money for the hospital would be a kind gesture. He figured that if any of the kids he coached ever got sick they would probably be admitted there so he felt there was a relevant connection.

Paul came up with the idea of running a black tie event, which he called the 'Wimbledon Ball'. His plan was to host a dinner that would coincide with the Wimbledon final, which played from 11 pm on TV. He admits he had no idea or plan for how to go about it, and he had plenty of sleepless nights in the lead-up. Luckily for Paul, he was coaching Belinda Green (who famously won Miss World in the 1970s). Belinda kindly offered to lend a hand with organising the event and said she asked Ray Martin (who was hosting the *Midday* show at the time) if he would host Paul's Wimbledon Ball. To Paul's great surprise and joy, Ray said yes! At that first event they raised $40 000.

Quite wisely, Paul made an appointment at RNSH to understand the needs of the hospital and said he would buy the equipment the hospital needed with the money raised at the Wimbledon Ball.

Paul continued to run the Wimbledon Ball, and by the sixth year they had raised a total of $700 000. After seeing brands such as Bandage Bear at the hospital, Paul decided it was time to get a brand to make his event more official. He talked to his network and came up with the name Humpty Dumpty Foundation (HDF).

Things didn't go so well when the head of paediatrics said they didn't like the name 'Humpty'. Needless to say, Paul was shattered. Nevertheless, he stayed the course. He contacted Ray Martin to discuss becoming more serious: creating a board, having a formal launch, and so on.

The annual ball continued and about six weeks after the sixth annual event Paul received a call from the head of paediatrics who apologised for making a mistake!

As Paul often says, 'Stay on the bus, or at least help steer it!'

Next, Paul decided to go to the hospital *before* the event to ask them what equipment they needed. It was an ingenious idea and was very well received. In addition to the prizes that were typically able to be won at events like these to raise donations, the hospital Wish List was born. This meant you could choose to buy a piece of equipment that had been directly requested by the hospital.

(*continued*)

HDF continued to grow and other hospitals began calling. Paul received a call from a nursing unit manager in the Hunter Valley (New South Wales) who told him that they did not have an EZ-IO drill (a $1500 piece of equipment) and that as a result they had lost a three-year-old child. She was in tears. This phone call started HDF's expansion outside of Sydney. Paul's call to arms was 'to support our cousins in the country'.

In the blink of an eye, HDF was going national! This hadn't been part of the plan until Joe Hockey (who was opposition treasurer at the time) went on Channel 7's *Sunrise* program to talk to David Koch about his plan to climb Mt Kilimanjaro in Tanzania to raise money for the HDF (he explained he had heard a nurse from a country town talk about a two-year-old child dying in her arms because the local hospital lacked a $1500 piece of equipment). David Koch said if it was a national charity, *Sunrise* could join the cause. As it turned out, David Koch joined the climb and *Sunrise* has been a long-term supporter of HDF ever since.

Paul always seeks feedback and when he heard that people didn't go to charity events because the food was often average or the wine was cheap, he made it his mission to ensure HDF's events had only the best food and that the wine was top quality.

HDF is a children's charity that, for more than 30 years, has been purchasing essential and often life-saving medical equipment for sick and injured children in paediatric wards, neonatal units, and maternity and emergency departments in hospitals across Australia. Through the Wish List and special projects, HDF has helped more than 500 hospitals and health service organisations improve their care of sick children.

HDF has now raised close to $100 million resulting in approximately 500 pieces of children's medical equipment being donated to hospitals and health services across Australia each year. This means that outside of state government, the HDF is the largest supplier of children's medical equipment in Australia.

> It is through Paul's determination and passion that HDF has been able to reach these heights, although Paul modestly asserts that 'anybody could do what I've done'.

Paul's journey may be a bit different from yours — maybe even extreme if you're sitting on the fence thinking about starting your giving journey and deciding where to put your first $20. But this story illustrates how you can make a real difference.

From a little seed, big things grow... and continue to grow.

Will giving ease your money worries?

Paul was passionate about helping save kids' lives. Money never came into it. Paul didn't come from wealth so he wasn't able to pour money into his passion. He had to work at it, in addition to working at his full-time job of coaching tennis. He wanted to make a difference and to make sure that his efforts would result in a positive outcome.

There is something so deeply satisfying about giving, that money worries don't seem to factor into the decision once you've made it. You do need to be sure though — it's not like you can get a refund!

The case for giving is a strong one and Paul would say it gives him the 'greatest pleasure'. There are huge emotional rewards, including joy and satisfaction. Giving has opened his eyes. Here's what Paul has learned from giving:

- Learning about different cultures in our community.
- Greater understanding of the needs of our indigenous families living in remote rural areas.
- Governance (how to run a charity).
- How to run a quality event and what matters to those who give.

- Empathy.
- The value of saying thank you.

If you're looking for more reasons to donate, take a look at this list of the most common experiences of giving:

- It's good for your health — a reliable wellness hit.
- It makes you feel happy and good.
- It promotes feelings of gratitude.
- It's contagious.
- It's more impactful than ever given that the world has seen so many natural disasters, COVID disruption and the global recovery from this.
- It teaches children the importance of generosity (more on that in chapter 14).
- You worry less about your own money worries by thinking of others.
- You get out of your own bubble.

If you are looking for another reason to start giving, my personal favourite is, 'You don't want to be the richest person in the cemetery'. This quote came directly from a road train driver in the Northern Territory and is a valuable reminder not to leave giving until it's too late!

What are the options for giving?

Making giving a habit is a worthwhile complement to your baseline costs (see chapter 1). The unique aspect to giving is that it can mean different things to different people. Whatever giving means to you, it should be considered a much bigger investment in your financial future because you are thinking about someone else's needs, not just your own. And when there are kids involved, it's great role modelling. Giving could be a financial goal (see chapter 2) for you as well.

Achieving this goal may have a compound effect on reducing your money worries.

Start by turning your mind to a cause that resonates with you. A story you might have heard, a 'feel-good' factor and a feeling of wanting to help should all come into it for you. This is when you know it's right for you to give.

Charities fulfil lots of different functions in society, providing emergency support and care for our most vulnerable, building social and community connections, responding to natural disasters and raising awareness of important issues. When you give money or your time to charities it has direct societal outcomes.

Charities love cash donations because they give them the flexibility to apply the much-needed cash direct to their cause. In most cases it's very simple to contribute as little as $2 to a charity of your choice. You can set up regular direct debits from your bank account as well if you'd like to consistently give money.

Go online to look for causes that you like, and consider which charities are aligned with your money values. You can also reassess where you give your money or make it something you consider annually. Enjoy the process of looking for a charity that connects with your heart and mind. It's worthwhile talking to members of your personal finance village as well. Donating online can be a bit of a minefield as there is so much choice.

For example, if you're looking for something aligned to helping others with financial worries, check out Kiva. It's a platform that crowdfunds microloans to lend money to low-income entrepreneurs and students to expand financial access to underserved communities around the world to help them thrive. You can help change lives.

For me, donating to a charity where I see a distinct connection between my donation and its intended mission, aligned with the charity's ethos, is one of the most valuable considerations when choosing a charity. In the case of HDF, for example, a donation buys a specific piece of equipment that saves lives. Not all charities can demonstrate the same direct connection with your giving.

Here's a list of things to consider when you're researching charities or organisations you might like to gift to:

- *Look at the charity's mission.* Does it connect with you? Does it interest you or do you share the same beliefs? It's important to have a connection as this builds the feel-good factor.

- *Look at the outcomes it is achieving.* Following the first point, be comfortable that the way the charity will spend your donation is aligned with their mission and makes sense to you.

- *Review any financial information to understand how much goes to its cause directly.* If you're not sure, ask them. You don't want to be paying for a fancy office or big salaries for people.

- *Understand who is on the board.* Understanding the board composition is your own barometer on the governance of the organisation. The board has a duty of care to ensure the charity delivers on its mission or purpose.

- *Are the charity's values aligned with your world views?* This relates to the first point. Giving is more enjoyable when you feel a connection.

- *Check in with your personal finance village.* Your PFV can help guide you in your choices, and might even be able to make suggestions to assist in decision making on which charity to support.

- *Make sure the charity is registered with the ACNC (Australian Charities and Not-for-profits Commission).* Check the ACNC charity register — an important part of your due diligence is knowing that it is a reputable and registered charity.

◆ *Search for status.* You can go a step further and search the ABN. Check their deductible gift recipients (DGR) status. A DGR is an organisation that has been registered to receive tax-deductible gifts. If you would like to make a tax-deductible donation to a charity, you have to ensure the charity is a DGR.

Finally, one of my favourite tips is, instead of buying gifts for family or friends for Christmas or birthdays, pick a charity that you think may be aligned to their interests. The one I like, particularly for young kids, is Oxfam. I recall a family member buying two goats (online of course) for my kids at Christmas to give to a family in Vanuatu. Oxfam helps families in crisis and poverty and enables you to buy chickens, goats, fish, ducks and cows. Oxfam also provides training and support to help families earn a living, so this is a great option to contribute to society in a fulfilling way.

It doesn't just have to be money that you give. Your time may be more valuable than money.

Let's spend a bit of time exploring other options for giving and gifting.

Time

Offering your skills as a volunteer might be one of the best ways you can contribute to a charity, especially if you want to help but you don't have the cash to spare. Indeed, the mere feeling of worry can be counteracted by thinking about others. (Thinking about others takes away from the focus on ourselves and relieves worry.)

Charities are like other businesses in that they need people to help across every aspect: finance, marketing, event management, strategy, web development, administration, shop assistants — you name it.

You might also be considering how you can help if you don't have any experience with working inside a charity. But it's your specific skillset that might be just what the charity needs and if you're passionate about what the charity is doing it's a win-win. When you look at Paul's journey, his own network was a really big help in getting HDF off the ground. Your network alone could also assist a charity if you know what they need. Don't be afraid to reach out if you believe in what they are doing or want to learn more. Most charities have a website that states their mission or vision.

You can volunteer from working in the soup kitchen to being a CEO.

Volunteering is a feel-good way to help. It's a little altruistic too: you may be making a sacrifice in terms of your time but giving regardless of the personal consequences.

Possessions

There is enough waste in the world and many charities have been established to ensure we minimise it. I'm sure you'll appreciate that not all waste is the same. With a little research you are likely to find a place for things you no longer need. Clutter in your home is an obvious one:

- clothes donations (this is the most popular type of charitable contribution)
- shoes and bags
- kitchenware
- books
- toys, games, sporting goods
- art
- linens
- hygiene essentials (e.g. toothpaste, deodorant, sanitary items, toilet paper)
- furniture.

Assets

You can consider bequeathing cash and/or property pursuant to your last Will and testament. It is a fairly simple process that involves:

1. asking a charity if they would be interested in accepting a donation from you

2. making and updating your Will.

Please do consult your personal finance village on this one. Your lawyer can help or can refer you to a specialist estate planning lawyer who can adjust your structure and will appropriately.

There are various forms of charitable bequest that you can make, and the gift will need to be included in the will. It can involve:

- the residuary of your estate after specific gifts have been made

- a percentage of the residue of your estate or a percentage of your entire estate

- a particular asset, including real estate, shares, bonds or other articles of value

- a specific sum of cash.

However, make sure you communicate your bequest wishes to your loved ones! We detailed the reasons why and how to do this properly in chapter 6. Communication will ensure your final wishes are carried out and don't create issues for anyone involved.

The joy of giving is when you're living so please do consider giving during your lifetime as well.

Trust distributions

As an alternative to making a cash donation, a distribution of income from a trust to a charitable organisation may be tax effective for you.

A valid income distribution from a trust to a beneficiary is subject to tax in the hands of the beneficiary at the beneficiary's income tax rate. Where a distribution is made to a registered charity, the distribution will be exempt from tax (but do check that your charity of choice is exempt from tax) and therefore no tax will be paid on the trust distribution.

Importantly, your charity of choice must be a beneficiary, or potential beneficiary, of the trust.

For example, if a trust has $10 000 of taxable income and distributes $4000 to a charity, it has a similar effect to making a tax-deductible donation of $4000, which would reduce the taxable income to $6000. Either way, the balance of taxable income is $6000.

Please note that many trust deeds include charities as a potential beneficiary and a trust distribution should be possible; however, it's important to obtain advice prior to your trust making the distribution to ensure that the distribution is permitted under the trust deed.

All trust distributions need to be documented prior to 30 June each financial year to give an effective present entitlement of trust income.

Options for giving as a business owner

As a business owner, looking for the most suitable option for giving is challenging. The global corporate movement known as Pledge 1% was formed in recognition of this. Businesses that belong to Pledge 1% do exactly that: they give 1 per cent of equity, staff time or product back to their communities, into charities or to causes of their choice. In essence, it's a company's way of giving back. Pledge 1% is an official way of committing to giving at the corporation level. Once you've made the commitment, you can engage your team in deciding where your pledge is best distributed. You may already work at a company that is a member.

There are a couple of reasons why pledging can bring a broader benefit:

- Your business can lead by giving.

- Customers are more likely to buy from a company that supports the broader community.

- It is appealing to prospective employees that there is a greater sense of purpose associated with the company. As an employee you might consider this to be a differentiator if you are comparing companies to work with. Culturally it may be more aligned with your values and give you more reasons to stay with your organisation.

- It's good for morale.

Pledge 1% is all about creating a positive social impact and is just one practical and organised way businesses can structure giving.

At the other end of the 'profit-for-purpose' spectrum are businesses such as Who Gives a Crap, which is known for selling 100 per cent recycled toilet paper and having a very clear mission. They donate a staggering 50 per cent of their profits to ensure everyone has access to clean water and a toilet. Now that's taking toilet paper sales to a whole new level!

Yvon Chouinard is another great example of profit-for-purpose. The billionaire founder of Patagonia took his moral obligation seriously. As a steward for de-growth economics (where you put wellbeing ahead of profit), together with his family, he gave their company to a cause close to their hearts: saving the planet. They were always committed to running a socially responsible business and they have now made good on this promise by creating a not-for-profit to combat climate change.

Impact investing

Impact investing is another way businesses can give. It achieves similar outcomes to charities. The key point of difference is the intention to make a profit (from the social or environmental impact) and return that to its shareholders. By way of contrast, a charity directs all its profit back to its cause.

Impact investing has become a focus of investors where they want to create positive and measurable social and environmental impact alongside a financial return. Impact investing is designed to address some of the world's most pressing challenges, such as sustainable agriculture, renewable energy, conservation, microfinance, and affordable and accessible basic services including housing, healthcare and education. In a positive way, impact investing challenges the long-held views that social and environmental issues should be addressed only by philanthropic donations, and that market investments should focus exclusively on achieving financial returns.

An easy option for employees

If the whole act of giving feels too complex to you, join an organisation (or investigate the one you're in) that has giving as a key pillar in its business and see how you can get involved with whatever it is doing. Today, most organisations adopt giving back as a key part of their strategy. Social impact is good corporate citizenship. They may give a percentage of the business earnings or they may offer skilled volunteering for people or businesses that would otherwise be unable to access those types of services. In addition, they are likely to have a workplace giving program so that you can contribute financial support (an amount goes out of your pay every month directly to charity) to different crises as they occur.

Get onboard with your research. Whether it's saving the planet, feeding the homeless or looking after wildlife, find a charity that works for you and decide what you can give.

Stop worrying now

1. Work out how you can contribute in a way that will ease your concerns and that works for you financially.

2. Consider the ways you might like to give. Is it through offering your time or skills to a charity that you like? If yes, what skills can you offer and does this charity suit your skills?

3. Do you want to make a difference but you don't have the time (and don't want to worry more)? It may ease your concerns and feel better for you to give some money, remembering that as little as $2 can make a difference. What will you commit to?

4. Make a list of the feel-good charity/ies that are connected with your values. You want giving to feel right for you.

Charity name	My donation
e.g. Two Good Co	Buy their cookbook for family for Christmas
	Set up direct debit for $5 a month
	Contact Two Good Co and offer to help out twice a month at their cafe

Chapter 14
Educate the next generation

My grandmother was a great savings role model. She managed the cash in the household and ran the family building and plumbing business from the living room while my grandfather went out and worked.

My recollection about their living style would today be considered frugal. Everything you earned and spent was a considered action. When you needed to buy anything, you had to go in to a bank branch and withdraw the cash from your bank account — no credit cards, no ATMs, no PayPal — so you really had to budget.

Money didn't fly out the door for online Amazon purchases and subscriptions. Clothes were made, not bought; mended rather than replaced. When the mail arrived, envelopes were saved for note making, writing shopping lists and phone messages. Calling from a landline (interstate) was a planned exercise for when Telstra had a cheaper rate per minute — for example, on Sunday nights between 6 and 8 pm — and you would time your phone call (it sounds funny even saying it now).

When I visited, we would have a Friday night, special, once-a-week trip to the local fish and chip shop to buy dinner (no Uber Eats).

Many family members would come together on a Sunday night for a roast (some still do). My main memory was not the meat of the day but the fry-up the next day or two where we would have the leftovers for dinner, maybe with an egg added. We called it 'bubble and squeak' (I dread to think how much oil that involved).

Things rarely went to waste. The cardboard from the Cornflakes box was kept; empty glass jars, soft drink bottles and milk bottles were recycled. It wasn't like we were poor; this was just how it was done. No generation since has lived through a depression. Food, supplies and work were scarce so you adjusted your way of living to conserve. The closest we have come since then may be the toilet paper shortages during the pandemic lockdowns, although this hardly qualifies for the type of adversity experienced by my grandparents.

When it came to gift giving, my grandmother slowly worked through every item we needed for school: a desk one year, a chair the next, a lamp, and so on… No junk, no trinkets — just practical and useful items. Also, birthdays were a celebration where you received something, but there was nothing in between birthdays and Christmas. (I always felt sorry for my uncle, who was born on Christmas day — he definitely drew the short straw.)

I absorbed these lessons like the giant sponge any impressionable 10-year-old is. I learned early how to be careful with money. I recognise now what a valuable start in life this provided, particularly to the development of my financial literacy. I also learned how to recycle, how to minimise waste, how to save my money, how to use it wisely and how to plan for spending. I wasn't growing up or living in a depression, but my grandparents had the experience of it and carried all the lessons with them throughout their lives.

People who lived through the Great Depression (1929–1939) and World War II (1939–1945) eras lived very differently from the way we do now. When you consider they endured skyrocketing costs of living and high unemployment, we could learn so much from them today because they had great insights into money management. What have we learned from them that we now pass on to our children? Think about how we live our lives differently from them and require different approaches to different challenges.

Generations since World War II have, and will continue to have, very different frameworks and economic climates to adapt to. There is a unique challenge for those of us born after this time. How do we continue to teach good money habits and get the balance right raising kids in today's affluent world? What do we teach them? How will we influence them growing up?

One of the greatest money worries is raising kids and money! We all want the best for our children, and we should be thinking about this. I am perplexed by the options for raising kids wisely about and around money. It doesn't matter if you are a grandparent, parent, aunty or cousin; we all have a responsibility to inspire the next generation to make better choices with money. It's also our duty as parents to teach as much as we can while we have (any) influence, so they don't end up in trouble, riddled with debt and making money mistakes. Teaching kids responsible money management provides a lasting legacy for future generations. You won't see this immediately, but I can tell you that, having witnessed money mistakes and issues being passed from generation to generation, the opportunity you have to change the direction and support better financial education for your kids is a worthwhile investment — possibly the best investment you will make in your lifetime.

Every time you click online to make a purchase, what are you teaching kids about money?

Be a role model

Teaching lessons or sharing your money experience with kids is an important part of role modelling and of children's development. A good financial role model doesn't complain about bills one day, then goes on a shopping spree the next. Once you do open up your money story, it's important to be aware of the mixed messages, however subtle you think they might be. Principally, kids need to see you demonstrating what you preach consistently. So, it's good to open up about money with them.

Parents are often reluctant to discuss financial topics with their kids for the following reasons:

- They are too young to understand.
- There are too many things to worry about right now.
- You are embarrassed about your own finances.
- You are concerned about household budget constraints.
- Maybe they will learn it at school.
- You are too stressed to take the time.
- You don't know enough.

However, in my experience kids are eager to learn more about money and wish their parents shared their wisdom sooner.

Financial literacy is not taught at school, but it should be.

We are missing a valuable opportunity to talk to kids about money. Home is the best place to learn and build your children's financial literacy.

Here's a list of what kids want you to share with them:

- How to save and spend money wisely.
- How much things cost.
- How to earn money.
- How to manage money.
- How to set financial goals.
- How to maintain a budget.
- How you run the family finances.

If it's news to you that your kids would like to know more about money, next time you click online or tap your card, walk your kids through the process. Start with something simple like the next purchase of your family pets' food (I'm thinking you might do this on a weekend at home around the kitchen table). If you're like me, you might have to do a price comparison first; this is all part of the experience for kids and it's great role-modelling. If you have pets, food is an essential item too so it's a life lesson for your kids. I won't miss the opportunity to point out how expensive dog food is (two lessons for the price of one): raising pets costs money as well as effort!

When credit card purchases go bad

One click on from your dog food purchase could be a request from your child for some money, or perhaps to use your credit card. Engaging kids in discussions about the use of money does require you to be money savvy. You can make it look too easy by clicking away, so it's best to follow up any spending chat with the source of funds conversation as well. If you hand over the card for a one-time-only purchase it could backfire, as it did in our house.

We had every online game in our house at one stage or another: Minecraft, Dofus, Clash of Clans, Call of Duty, League of Legends, FIFA and of course Fortnite. When one of our sons, Max, was about 10 years old and at the stage where his fixation on online gaming was near its peak, he pestered us about buying some 'V-Bucks' (more generally known as in-game currencies or micro transactions) to help improve the cosmetics of his avatars in the game. We understood that these V-Bucks would also improve the gaming experience with his mates online (I use the term 'mates' loosely – I'm referring to kids around the world playing at the same time). We suggested that if he helped with a few chores around the house and kept his room tidy we would agree to help with the purchase (which was about $5). Little did we know at the time, our credit card details were saved in the autofill of the game itself!

Luckily, ever the credit card statement reviewer, I was looking at the Visa statement and I saw lots of small transactions of $5 and $10 — they totalled more than $700 in one month (that's a lot of fivers)!

Is this why two-factor authentication was invented? It might have saved me $700 — but then we wouldn't have learned a couple of valuable lessons:

- The games are designed to suck kids right in.

- They are also designed to capture your attention for their profit.

- The more V-Bucks you bought, the greater the addiction to play and buy more (scary).

- Just because it's a secure payment method doesn't mean you should give your credit card details to just anyone.

- Max had to pay back the $700 in household chores — no bail outs.

- The experience opened a new conversation for us at home about how these games are designed.

- Reminder — check your statements!

We all want to protect our kids, and this is a great example of how it's too easy to spend money initially without realising there are consequences. These games become egregious when you can't compete at a higher level unless you buy some of the in-game currencies, as is the case now with FIFA.

A survey — conducted by YouGov for the CBA — of Australian adults with children aged eight to 17 years found that 50 per cent had spent their parents' money without the parent knowing. Alarmingly, 56 per cent of parents had caught their children spending without permission. In-app purchases were the highest spend, followed by online shopping.

As kids get older, it becomes more sophisticated. Before you know it, they are gambling online and end up in debt and likely coming to you to be saved.

The last thing you, or any parent, wants to be doing is lying awake at night worrying about where their kids are, what they're doing or if they're getting into trouble — or whether they might be spending your money!

We have to set kids up with the right mindset and tools so that they understand and are financially savvy in today's world.

Max was kind of lucky (only in the sense that he learned this lesson relatively early in life) that we realised he was inhaling Fortnite V-Bucks while the Bank of Mum and Dad took care of the bill. He was a little too young to go and get a job to repay his $700 so he did have to rely on the Bank of Mum and Dad. You might ask yourself, when are the kids too old to see the Bank of Mum and Dad as an option? I think the answer is, there is no time in your life when you want to find out that you are or have become the bank for your kids.

It's never too soon to start

A child's curiosity is a wonderful thing, and you can take baby steps by explaining the money world to them. Pick something simple and show them how it works. Everyday situations are a great learning ground. It's your responsibility as a parent to send them into the world with good money habits, which is a win-win for everyone.

We need to build their knowledge so that kids understand financial concepts, and risks, and to give them the skills, motivation and confidence so they can make informed judgements about the use and management of money.

Here are some things to be mindful of:

- *Earning money.* Natural curiosity, of course, will lead kids to wonder where the money tree is once they see you tapping away. Explain to them that when you go off to work you get paid. This money replenishes your bank account and that money gets used for all the essentials the family needs, such as food, clothing and, of course, your family home.

- *Tapping your credit card or phone.* When buying groceries, explain that when you are tapping the card it talks to your bank account, where you keep your savings. You can also explain that each time you tap, money is going out of your bank account (we'll get to this in a moment), using your savings, so you need to earn more money to replenish it.

- *Explaining bank accounts.* Showing your kids that bank accounts are a place for you to deposit and withdraw funds, make payments, transfer money to another person or institution, pay bills electronically — and more — is important. Bank accounts enable you to spend without cash on hand and get direct deposits from employers or other institutions.

- *Checking prices.* Show your kids different bags of rice on the supermarket shelf. Explain the different prices and how you go about choosing to buy the one with the best value or deal (if a brand has been discounted). Then, once you have paid, show them the receipt with the price listed on it. By showing them the receipt, you can demonstrate the transition from the shelf onto the docket (receipt) and explain that this amount will come out of your bank account.

- *Paying bills.* Keep it simple and relevant: a good place to start might be your mobile phone or internet bill. Most kids will be familiar with a device or two now so you can show them that to play games at home or for them to use their iPad at home, you need to pay for the internet. Show them a bill and then walk them through the steps for paying, similarly to the rice scenario.

- *Ordering a school lunch.* From the age of four or five, kids are entering school and might be able to buy their lunch or a special treat. Use this as a stepping stone. If you are giving them money, you can explain where that money came from. If your child's school has an online ordering system, go onto the website and step through what you are doing so they can order their lunch.

- *Being aware of risk.* It's not too early to let kids know about scammers and maybe give an example of a phone call you might have received, explaining the risks with giving personal details over the phone or online. It's easy to hold off explaining this so you don't frighten your kids or freak them out, but perhaps this is a critical awareness for kids today — stranger danger in a finance story. It needs to be told.

- *Explaining the use of lay-by and after-pay options.* The former is a great mechanism for saving towards a goal and the latter is a slippery slope to debt. Encourage kids to understand the types of options available for spending money:

  - Lay-by agreements let you buy a product and pay for it in two or more instalments before taking it home. It's important for kids to understand what the written agreement covers and how you or the business you are buying from can cancel it.

  - Afterpay is a buy now, pay later lender (similar to Klarna or Affirm) that divides your total purchase amount into four bi-weekly payments. If a retailer uses Afterpay, you can leave the store with your item or order it online after putting down just 25 per cent of the total price.

Create good money habits early.

The teen money journey and beyond

Financial literacy and knowhow is crucial for teens. Having and building their financial skills will have a huge impact on their financial success or failure stepping into adulthood. Teens do keep us all awake at night. They can be troublesome at an age where hormones are crazy, and friendships can be lifelines or shipwrecks. They can work outside the home and be paid, giving them their first taste of financial independence — even the financial freedom to spend without consequence or without you knowing about it. They might get behind a wheel... Just writing this paragraph raises my anxiety levels!

Starting their money journey early is good for them and good for you. Learning the Fortnite lesson early has saved our family from the trappings of these games to a large extent. Now in his late teens, with the arrival of the latest FIFA game, Max can discernibly choose *not* to buy the FIFA points or packs to get better players. Like all things, the prices are higher now and you can spend $1 or $100 to build your perfect soccer team. Imagine the cost of the perfect soccer team appearing on your next statement — ouch! Check your credit card statements. (I know I've said this before, but it's important.)

The sooner we get started, the greater the chance of avoiding these kinds of issues.

There's no question that the sooner you get the kids involved, the better. No doubt they will make better choices as they begin to learn the value of money. They are likely to recognise it needs planning and consideration. As they transition through the teen years and realise they can start to earn money themselves and what they might be able to do with it, you can work with them, guiding them to develop and achieve specific money goals.

There are three key roles of money you need to teach your kids:

1. Earning

2. Spending

3. Saving.

Let's look at each one.

Earning

The sooner kids learn the concept of *earning* money, the sooner you can have savings conversations with them.

However, you have to learn to run before you can walk, so learning how to earn is the necessary precursor to saving! Here are some things to consider.

POCKET MONEY

Pocket money is a great starting point. To earn it and create good money habits you must first establish what tasks the kids can take on. Some typical household tasks include walking the dog, mowing the lawn, washing the car and hanging out the washing.

Kids might baulk at this, but if they don't do the agreed task, it's wise to reduce their pocket money so that you create the expectation that a job done properly is the one you get paid for.

We've tried many versions of pocket money to try and get the right balance and the more kids you have, the harder this gets, in my view. You don't want to feel like a police officer every time you walk into the house. We eventually took the stance that some things are simply part of being a family and so our sons didn't get paid for chores like tidying their rooms. You have to weigh up the pros and cons for your family and make sure by doing this you are clear on your family values and goals and the relationship to money. If your kids are earning pocket money on an 'easy come' basis, what will they learn? What kind of standard are you setting?

What we did pay them for was for something out of the 'norm', like helping in our businesses — such as planting 300 trees on the farm, helping dig holes for fence posts, bagging cow manure for grandma, cleaning our business office (that's what being a part of the family business looks like). There was a bigger picture here too: being able to show the kids that the different aspects and machinations of the business was good for their overall development, from developing their work ethic, to understanding how to earn money (and what you earn per hour) for doing *real* work.

When the kids work in the family business, they get to see a much clearer link between their activity (i.e. work) and how they *earn* money.

ALLOWANCE

Allowances are often used by parents with the intention of creating some money responsibility. If an allowance is given without children learning to earn the money, what is your child taking away from this? The problem with an allowance is that it creates a pattern or expectation about money that's not real. This pattern is not entirely appealing. When you decide to stop the allowance, what will be your reasoning?

In some circumstances, allowances are okay when there is expectation that your child does certain chores to earn it (similarly to the list above).

PART-TIME JOB

This is 100 per cent my personal favourite. It's easier for someone else to be the boss of your child! They seem to take feedback better that way and it takes all the noise out of the house when you are arguing about the five-minute dog walk that should have been 20 minutes (yes, I've had this argument).

MATCH IT

In addition to the earning options above, you could consider a 'matching' principle. By way of example, you can match every $10 earned *and* saved by your child to double their savings. This is a 'special occasions' type of earner. It's not something I would consider often, but it does help delay gratification and influence savings as well as considered spending. Money can burn a hole in kids' pockets (they can be desperate to spend it as soon as they have earned it) so having a conversation about something they really want and offering to match their savings has them setting a goal as well.

Spending

The tectonic financial shift that has occurred over the past few decades is our need for instant gratification and how it has impacted our spending. We are now well trained to expect things *now — stat!* Whether it's fast food, fast purchases, Amazon arriving the day you click online or immediate connectivity with our 'network' online, there's no waiting. In this day and age, it is upon us as parents to help our children delay gratification, as with the 'match it' principle above. It's easy to feel like the chips are stacked against you with the likes of Afterpay business models hovering over your every click and explaining to your kids that every click hurts!

Again, it's just another important lesson in the journey to financial enlightenment for our kids. Your role modelling on spending is most important. If your kids see you with colourful shopping bags, or packages arriving at the front door weekly or even daily, you're not necessarily setting a good example unless you can demonstrate that your spending is within your means, or within a budget, and you don't go on moaning about bills down the track.

> **The journey to saving is a key part in helping delay gratification for spending (for them as well as us!).**

Saving

Saving is a fundamental money habit; one we all need to learn. Saving teaches you discipline in the long run. Saving builds your security and financial independence (aka helps you stop worrying). Explaining to your kids how and why you save your earnings is ideal. Saving money for emergencies is another good reminder for us all. Little emergencies pop up, such as a broken dishwasher, and can help kids understand that having some money set aside is valuable. Imagine having to wash dishes!

Also, don't miss the opportunity with younger kids, when they get some birthday money (such as a cash gift from the relos), to give them a glass jar and call it a piggy bank. Make it visible. Explain that it is like a bank account. When they are older, they can take the money they saved to the bank and deposit it as savings.

By saving money, young kids are focused on short-term goals such as a toy or the latest PlayStation game. The older they get, the more likely you are to be addressing newer influences such as their pay cheque and how they want to dress, because up to a point you will have always 'dressed' your kids.

You can readily explain that you can't spend unless you have *saved*.

Once kids understand they can save, you can then teach them about investing as an alternative to spending. Begin with the virtues of compound interest; that usually gets their attention. Teaching kids to save, then invest, will have them well on the track to financial independence as adults and minimise any money worries in your combined futures. If investing is not your strength, then by all means help your kids find an online course, buy your kids a book to introduce them to investing, or consider introducing them to your personal finance village or someone who can give them some guidance on the basic principles of investing. This also encourages them to seek advice before they invest. This is an important aspect to your own legacy.

While you're taking your kids on the journey to saving, how about sitting down with them and explaining all the reasons for saving and getting them to consider on their own what they might want to save for. It's hard for kids to think longer term and we all need to be patient with this.

The process is intended to delay gratification, rather than encourage immediate spending. Sit down and complete this table alongside them. I've given you a few suggestions to get you started.

Adult's reason for saving	Child's reason for saving
Freedom to pursue a different career	*For a new PlayStation game*
To go on a nice holiday	*To buy a souvenir on the family holiday*
For longer term financial security	
To invest to earn passive income	*To buy a car when I'm older*
To reduce stress	
To give to a good cause	*To donate to kids in need*

Activities to develop financial literacy

Once your kids have grasped the three roles of money, you can progress to these three key activities to further develop their financial literacy:

1. Creating goals

2. Budgeting

3. Giving.

Creating goals

You can help your child set money goals. This definitely aids with delayed gratification. Instead of their savings burning a hole in their pocket, you can further encourage them to pause for a while, and maybe check if their money goal is big enough. Look over their list (see above). Do they need to save more before they spend up? What about investing their money, watching it grow and then reconsidering whether or not to spend it down the track?

Get them to test their need to spend now. Would they rather buy the new shoes now or wait until later for the newer model or new season?

I am a fan of offering to match or offer a 'bonus' for reaching money savings/goals, as I mentioned earlier.

Getting your kids to recognise the trade-offs is another technique. Helping separate needs from wants can be a real challenge for kids (and us at times).

Establishing savings goals helps build a little bit of money resilience, which will make life easier for them as adults.

Budgeting

Why not get the kids involved in the family budgeting process? I'm sure they've heard you moan about bills such as electricity on occasion, or car regos, which seem to come around far too quickly. Bring them into the loop: take them back to chapter 1 and show them your budget.

If this feels too big, go with something smaller. Say you are going on a family holiday and you agree to give the kids a budget: let's say $100. Every time they want to get a juice or a souvenir, they need to work that into their budget for the duration of your stay. I think this works well when buying gifts or doing Christmas shopping as well.

Learning that it's not how much you make but what you do with what you make makes all the difference.

LIVING WITHIN YOUR MEANS: FOR YOUNG ADULTS

Living within your means can be a challenging topic to raise with young adults when the Bank of Mum and Dad is at their disposal.

I recommend encouraging them to budget their own outgoings and setting aside money for investment or emergencies.

As with all money habits, being a good role model helps here too.

Giving

It's never too early to introduce philanthropy to kids. Kids seem quite interested in giving once they understand the needs of others. Initially, you might just be teaching your kids that they can share money with others. Later you can provide an option for giving to help others less fortunate than them.

I was introduced to Meals on Wheels when I was young. I used to go along with my mum when she collected the food and delivered it to older people who were still living in their homes. It was certainly an eye opener for me seeing this and understanding how lonely they were and that it was really difficult for them to cook due to lack of mobility and other issues. I have no doubt this helped develop my empathy and an appreciation for my mum's generosity in giving her time. I'm sure my mum would say 'charity begins at home' and I think this is a great motto. I learned early that we have a responsibility to help others.

Red flags to watch for

Entitlement is a big concern for parents. Raising children today is hard but raising an un-entitled child is even more difficult no matter how much money you have or haven't got.

Entitlement has always existed; however, our level of affluence seems to exponentially increase the risk that kids come off entitled.

What do I mean by this? And has your child got affluenza? In the context of children and wealth, entitlement is when someone has a belief that they are inherently deserving of certain privileges or special treatment—that is, they believe they have a right to get whatever they want.

When it comes to money, not being accountable can spell danger for kids. Entitlement comes in many forms. The toddler version of entitlement is a three-year-old mega tantrum on the supermarket floor when you say *no* to buying the toy or colourful snack on the shelf! This is the start of it. Okay, it might seem a little tongue in cheek: to be clear, three year olds don't have emotional intelligence yet because their brains are still developing. The issue to watch out for, though, is if you succumb to the tantrum and buy the box of fruit loops, what are you showing your kids? What type of behaviour are you demonstrating? Is this the best money role model you can be?

A tantrum is verging on (or actually is) entitlement. It's the kind of reaction you might get from an entitled teen — or worse, a young adult — when you say *no* to buying everything on their long Christmas list, or *no* to loaning them money or *no* to bailing them out of some financial difficulty. Or even back to basics, refusing to pay for Uber Eats when there are perfectly good leftovers in the fridge.

Here are some worrying signs there's a case of affluenza with your child:

+ They can't delay gratification and can't take no for an answer. They want what they want right now, and they're willing to go to war with you every time.

+ They won't work. They always have some reason why they can't help with chores or finish a difficult assignment.

+ They expect parents to rescue them from forgetfulness and failure. They believe someone will help finish their homework, bring them their lunch at school and generally make up for any mistakes they make in life. Why be responsible when you know your parents will bail you out?

+ They don't show or feel gratitude.

+ They are more concerned about themselves than others.

+ They pass on blame when things go wrong and they can't handle disappointment.

Beware. Research shows entitlement in young people is on the increase and it can lead to a cycle of disappointment, anger, negativity and a constant need for that person to tell themselves that they are special. Entitlement grows slowly.

We all want the best for our kids. Naturally we want to give them everything we can, right? We know it starts off small, with the toy in the supermarket, then grows to clothing and technology for teens, then to motor vehicles and on and on. It's important to try and curb affluenza in your home as the consequences for you and your growing child can be very serious.

You have to take a long-term view, and accept the short-term pain to reduce the likelihood of developing affluenza in your family. No matter what age or stage your children are at, here are some universally proven options to help curb affluenza in your home:

- Say *no*. Full stop.

- Give kids specific jobs in the family and make it clear that when they do the work, they get the full payment. This has to be carefully balanced, with your child not expecting to be paid every time you ask them to do something.

- Failure: possibly the hardest thing for a parent to do is to let your child fail but it becomes a most valuable lesson in life.

- Accountability: let the lessons be learned (e.g. Max and the $700 bill). Let them make a mistake and work their way back from it with your guidance, not your bank account.

- Thank you: teach your child to say thanks and be grateful so they understand how lucky they are.

- Last resort: give your money away. You could take a leaf out of some of the world's rich listers' books. If you'd like to reduce your children's feelings of entitlement to your money, you can plan to give it away rather than leaving it to them (to a philanthropic cause of course!).

But remember: your relationship with your kids must come first. Building their financial literacy comes after that.

Your legacy is developing today's kids into wise adults who don't worry about money like you might have. Not because you gave them your money but because you took them on the money journey and helped create a positive money story they can develop over time (by arming them with the tools in this book), leading to a secure financial future.

Stop worrying now

1. Pick a moment to pop into your kid's room or wait until you're sitting at the dinner table. Tell them that you've just finished reading this chapter about kids and money and share your reflections.

2. Tell them what lessons you have learned.

3. Then ask your kids what they want to know about money. What do they want to learn about money (that's a good place to start the conversation at home)?

4. Consider, next time you're spending money, how you can engage the kids in the decision process.

5. The next dinner table topic could be the family budget and how you go about putting it together!

What next?

My intention with this book was to share practical stories and techniques to help you stop worrying about money and start planning *now* to secure your financial future.

Life is full of ups, downs, setbacks and the occasional U-turn, and you might have had a rough time. It's really important that you recognise those mistakes as learning experiences in your life. They are part of your developing money journey as you continue to look forward with a positive approach to creating a money story that delivers on your goals, no matter how large or small they are.

So whatever stage you are at right now in your life, draw a line in the sand. Get your house in order. Reset your goals. Address those baseline costs. Make changes to your spending.

We know money is a dynamic and transitional part of our lives, and it is likely to be changing all the time, so don't get complacent. It's not a set-it and forget-it process. We know from experience that your baseline costs will continue to change, but keep an eye on the creep, no matter whether you move, start a business, change relationships or for some other reason.

Remember to talk about money at home, with your partner, friends and kids. Normalise it and help others with their financial literacy if you can. The more we all know, the better off we will be.

It's never too late to turn your money worries around. You need to own them and stop worrying by using the skills and tools in this book to help you.

Whatever you choose to do next, I'll be here.

Jacqui

Connect with me

Thank you for taking the time to read this book. I hope it's been, and continues to be, immensely valuable.

Throughout the book are many practical templates, tools and exercises to help you get your house in order and plan your future. I encourage you to revisit these as your life and finances change. If you need to revisit any of the templates in this book, you can download them directly from my website: jacquiclarke.me

You can keep in touch with me here:

Website: jacquiclarke.me

Email: jc@jacquiclarke.me

Jacqui

Acknowledgements

This book was written between Gadigal land on Eora Country, and Yuin Nation on Walbanga Country.

Thank you to my village. This book would not have happened without your support.

To my husband Michael for your unwavering support and encouragement, and for challenging me to get it right. For reading my drafts … and drafts … Thank you for your patience and for helping me to stay the course when I wobbled.

Our sons, Jack, Joel, Harry, Max and Max (that's not a typo), you are my inspiration for this book. I appreciated your fun money stories and filling in the gaps in my memory. Thank you for your understanding during the writing process.

Nan (my mother-in-law): thank you for your first thoughts and comments on the book proposal as it was coming to life and your support and encouragement along the way.

My parents Colin and Sue: for being great parents and role models for a happy marriage and partnership!

Vashti Whitfield, my globally acclaimed coach. Thank you for your passion in bringing clarity to my vision for living life aligned with my values and giving birth to the idea that a book (at least one) must be written!

Kelly Irving: the best book coach. For your calm and direct style to guide me to writing a book and squeezing the nuggets out of the facts. A huge thank you also goes to your Expert Author Academy, a community of amazing, talented authors. A very special acknowledgement to Melo Calarco and Karen Stein, who kindly adopted me into their book-writing pod.

Lucy Raymond: for recognising that this book needed to be written and providing the support needed to commit Wiley to publish my book.

Thank you to my friends, clients and colleagues who helped sprinkle a little fairy dust and inspiration on every part of my book-writing journey, including: Jamie Pride, Janine Garner, Robert Joske, General the Honourable Sir Peter Cosgrove AK AC (Mil) CVO MC (Retd), Giam Swiegers, Jody Boshoff, Tom Gilliatt, Paul Fudge, Paul Francis (OAM), Will Hamilton, Juliet Bourke, the Smithams, Mandy Tsang, Ike Levick, Leigh McLennon and Sandra Balonyi.

And lastly, thank you to my Peloton bike, for keeping me sane and fit while I was sitting at a desk, day in and day out.

Where to go for help

We've covered some complex money issues and identified some worrying money situations where things can escalate quickly. There are organisations trained to deal with some of the emotional and tricky subjects this book has touched on, so please seek qualified and professional help for any of these situations.

Gambling

Gambling Help Online: gamblinghelponline.org.au

Wesley Mission: wesleymission.org.au

Reach Out: au.reachout.com

Gamblers Anonymous: gaaustralia.org.au

Smart Recovery: smartrecoveryaustralia.com.au

Salvation Army: salvos.org.au

Call Gambling Help Online on 1800 858 858 for free 24/7 telephone counselling.

Call the Financial Counselling Hotline on 1800 007 007 for assistance with financial difficulties.

Speak to a telephone counsellor at Lifeline on 13 11 14 for 24/7 support with any personal difficulties or distress.

Local states have many resources as well, such as GambleAware in New South Wales: gambleaware.nsw.gov.au

Addiction

National Alcohol and Other Drug Hotline: 1800 250 015

Turning Point: turningpoint.org.au/treatment/about-addiction/ counsellingonline.org.au

Financial abuse

White Ribbon Australia: whiteribbon.org.au

1800RESPECT: 1800respect.org.au/violence-and-abuse/financial-abuse/toolkit

Redfern Legal Centre: rlc.org.au/our-services/financial-abuse-service-nsw

Commonwealth Bank of Australia: commbank.com.au/content/dam/commbank-assets/about-us/2019-04/financial-abuse.pdf

Australian Human Rights Commission: humanrights.gov.au/our-work/5-your-right-be-free-financial-abuse

Elder abuse

National Elder Abuse Helpline: 1800 353 374

Older Persons Advocacy Network: opan.org.au

Elder Abuse Action Australia: eaaa.org.au

Better Place Australia: betterplaceaustralia.com.au

Sources

Chapter 2

Bonnie Barker, 2020, 'Driver or passenger: how recessions impact young Australian workers', EY, 29 June.

Brian Kropp and Emily Rose McRae, 2022, '11 trends that will shape work in 2022 and beyond', HBR, 13 January.

Chapter 3

Bonnie Barker, 2020, 'Driver or passenger: how recessions impact young Australian workers', EY, 29 June.

Chapter 4

'Give Me Shelter' report: Women aged 55 and over are the fastest-growing cohort of homelessness in Australians with an increase of 31% between 2011–2016, HAA.

Chapter 5

Joshua Becker, 2022, *Things that matter*, Penguin Random House.

Katie Canales and Katie Balevic, 2019, 'The Mega Millions jackpot is now the second largest in history. Here are disappointing stories that reveal what it's really like to win the lottery.', *Business Insider*. Accessed 12 January 2023.

Sarah Wilson, 2021, 'In the early days of Covid-19, we stopped consuming and rather loved it. But it didn't stick', *The Guardian*. Accessed 12 January 2023.

Chapter 6

'Glossary of terms', 2022, NSW Government. Accessed 12 January 2023.

Chapter 11

Welcome, n.d., ASBFEO. Available at: https://www.asbfeo.gov.au/. Accessed: 12 January, 2023.

Chapter 12

Regional Australia Institute, 2022, 'Regional Movers Index: June 2022 Quarter Report'. Available at: https://regionalaustralia.org.au/common/Uploaded%20files/Files/Regional%20Movers%20Index/Regional-Movers-Index-June-2022-Report.pdf. Accessed 12 January 2023.

'Are you ready for a sea change?', n.d., Sea Change Success. Accessed 12 January 2022.

Chapter 13

Centre for Social Impact, 2022, 'High net wealth giving in Australia: a review of the evidence', August.

Home, 2023, ACNC. Available at: https://www.acnc.gov.au/. Accessed January 12, 2023.

ABN Lookup, 2014, Australian Government. Department of Industry. Available at: https://abn.business.gov.au/. Accessed January 12, 2023.

'Emotions of giving: The cost of kindness', n.d., World Vision. Accessed 12 January 2022.

'Make a loan, change a life', n.d., Kiva. Accessed 12 January 2022.

'The future is equal', n.d., Oxfam International. Accessed 12 January 2022.

Chapter 14

'13th annual parents, kids & money survey', 2022, T. Rowe Price. Available from: https://www.moneyconfidentkids.com/content/dam/mck/pdfs/2021_Final_PKM_Deck_2022_Update.pdf

Greg Evans, 2017, 'Psychologists say more and more young people are entitled', indy100. Accessed 12 January 2022.

Index